DAVID DAUBE
A CENTENARY CELEBRATION

David Daube
A Centenary Celebration

❧

A collection of essays presented in memory
of David Daube, a scholar of Roman and
Biblical Law, on the hundredth
anniversary of his birth

Edited by
Ernest Metzger

Glasgow · Traditio Iuris Romani · MMX

© Ernest Metzger and the Contributors, 2010.

Published by Traditio Iuris Romani. Enquiries to Ernest Metzger, The University of Glasgow School of Law, Glasgow G12 8QQ, United Kingdom.

Works published under this imprint are partnered with *Roman Legal Tradition*, a periodical published by the Ames Foundation at the Harvard Law School and the University of Glasgow School of Law. ISSN 1943-6483. ROMANLEGALTRADITION.ORG

A catalogue record for this book is available from the British Library.

ISBN 978-0-9566423-0-1

The right of the contributors to be identified as authors of this work has been asserted in accordance with the Copyright, Designs and Patents Act 1988.

Contents

I. David Daube Centenary   1

    DAVID CAREY MILLER, Professor of Property Law Emeritus, University of Aberdeen

II. David Daube and T. B. Smith   11

    HECTOR L. MACQUEEN, Professor of Private Law, University of Edinburgh

III. David Daube on Causation in the Bible   37

    ROBERT A. SEGAL, Sixth Century Professor of Religious Studies, University of Aberdeen

IV. Jacob's 'Red, Red Dish' and the Riddle of the Red Heifer   48

    CALUM CARMICHAEL, Professor of Comparative Literature and Adjunct Professor of Law, Cornell University

V. Law, Narrative and Theology: Daube on the Prodigal Son   71

    BERNARD JACKSON, Professor of Law and Jewish Studies, Liverpool Hope University

(Continued overleaf.)

| VI. | David's Teaching in Aberdeen | 88 |

WILLIAM M. GORDON, Douglas
Professor of Civil Law Emeritus,
University of Glasgow

| VII. | Remarks on David Daube's Lectures on Sale, with Special Attention to the *liber homo* and *res extra commercium* | 101 |

ERNEST METZGER, Douglas Professor
of Civil Law, University of Glasgow

| VIII. | David Daube: A Personal Reminiscence | 127 |

ALAN WATSON, Distinguished
Research Professor and Ernest P.
Rogers Chair of Law, University of
Georgia School of Law

| IX. | David Daube | 138 |

JONATHAN M. DAUBE, President
Emeritus of Manchester Community
College, Manchester, Connecticut;
President of the University of
Aberdeen Development Trust USA

'You always say something different.'

— The Daube children to their father
(*Jottings of David Daube*, p. 45)

I

David Daube Centenary

David Carey Miller*

The author discusses the centenary celebration of David Daube's birth in the context of Daube's broad and enduring legacy at the University of Aberdeen.

Over the 27th and 28th of February 2009 the University of Aberdeen held a conference to celebrate the centenary of the birth, on 8 February 1909, of David Daube, a scholar of exceptional brilliance and diversity who worked with equal insight and originality on legal and theological texts. A refugee from Nazi Germany, Daube taught Roman law at Cambridge[1] before appointment as the first Professor of Jurisprudence at Aberdeen in 1951; less than five years later Daube accepted an invitation to take up the Regius Chair of Civil Law at Oxford which had become vacant on the unexpected death of Professor H. F. Jolowicz. In 1970 Daube moved to the University of California, Berkeley, to become Professor-in-Residence and Director of the Robbins Hebrew and Roman Law Collection. David Daube died on 24 February 1999. The conference programme brought together scholars who were

---

* Emeritus Professor of Property Law, University of Aberdeen; Senior Associate Research Fellow, Institute of Advanced Legal Studies, London. I am grateful to Dr Angus Campbell and to my wife Anne MacKenzie for reading and commenting on drafts of this piece; neither is responsible for its flaws and failings.

[1] For invaluable detail on this and other aspects of Daube's life, see A. Rodger, 'David Daube (8.2.1909 – 24.2.1999)', *Zeitschrift der Savigny-Stiftung für Rechtsgeschichte*, romanistische Abteilung, 118 (2001), xiv; see also A. Rodger, 'David Daube (1909 – 1999)', in J. Beatson and R. Zimmermann, eds., *Jurists Uprooted: German-speaking Émigré Lawyers in Twentieth-century Britain* (Oxford 2004), 233.

taught by Daube as well as those acquainted with him through his work.

The seed for this conference was sown by an earlier Aberdeen University event. On 2 November 2001 the first CMS Cameron McKenna lecture was given by Lord Rodger of Earlsferry in honour of David Daube.

The CMS Cameron McKenna lecture series came into being through the idea of Alexander Green, a 1980s student and my comparative law class prize winner. In the late 1990s, as a CMS Cameron McKenna partner, he suggested an annual lecture, to honour Aberdeen legal scholars who had contributed in a major way. The series has been a great success. In 2006, when Alex Green commenced practice on his own account, the series became 'The Alexander Green Law Agency Lectures'.

It was a very easy decision that the first of these lectures should be in recognition of the exceptional work and contribution of David Daube. The roll of subsequent scholars honoured tells something of the Aberdeen University Law School's twentieth-century strength to which David Daube's relatively short tenure was of disproportionately positive significance.

Briefly to bring up-to-date the lecture series story, subsequent CMS Cameron McKenna lectures honoured Peter Stein (5 July 2002, lecturer Reinhard Zimmermann: 'Remedies for Breach of Contract'[2]); T. B. Smith (7 November 2003, lecturer Kenneth Reid: 'While One Hundred Remain: T. B. Smith and the Progress of Scots Law'[3]); and A. E. Anton (29 March 2005, double bill lecture, Lord Justice Mance (as he then was): 'The Future of Private International Law in Europe'[4] and Paul Beaumont: 'The Work and Contribution of Professor A. E. Anton in the Field of Private International Law'[5]). The first Alexander Green Law Agency Lecture, in honour of William

---

[2] See R. Zimmermann, *The New German Law of Obligations* (Oxford 2005), ch. 2.
[3] See K. Reid, 'While One Hundred Remain: T. B. Smith and the Progress of Scots Law', in E. Reid and D. L. Carey Miller, eds., *A Mixed Legal System in Transition* (Edinburgh 2005), 1.
[4] See Lord Mance, 'The Future of Private International Law', *Journal of Private International Law*, 1 (2005), 185.
[5] See P. Beaumont, 'The Contribution of Alexander (Sandy) Anton to the Development of Private International Law', *Juridical Review* (2006), 1.

Gordon, a contributor to this volume, was given by Roddy Paisley (2 March 2009, on the subject 'Keeping Law Alive: Imponderables in Succession Law').

Coming back to the 2001 lecture which, as I have said, was the progenitor of the 2009 David Daube Centenary conference, Alan Rodger's title, *Law for All Times*, was a most fitting one in terms of the enduring character of Daube's contribution.

Proceedings were opened by Professor Paul Beaumont, the then Head of School. Lord Hope of Craighead was in the Chair. The text of the first CMS Cameron McKenna lecture given on 2 November 2001 and articles based on some of the papers given at a colloquium held on the following day are published in a volume edited by Ernest Metzger,[6] since 2006 the Douglas Professor of Civil Law at Glasgow, formerly holder of a personal chair of Civil and Comparative Law at Aberdeen.

Observing David Daube's capacity to make highly perceptive use of his vast store of knowledge on a whole range of subjects and 'put particular situations into a much wider framework and so to give the commonplace a much greater significance',[7] Alan Rodger showed how Daube's inaugural lecture at Aberdeen on the Scales of Justice gave valuable critical insights into contemporary justice issues. Peter Stein and John Shand in *Legal Values in Western Society*,[8] pointing out that both civil and criminal processes 'sometimes make justice seem subservient to the rules of the legal game',[9] refer to Daube's presentation of the judgment-of-Solomon problem in the published version of his Aberdeen inaugural lecture.[10]

Turning to the focus of Daube's talents in his interpretation of texts — 'surely the hallmark of all David's scholarly work' — Alan Rodger said that '[v]irtually all of that work revolves round the detailed and sensitive analysis of the

---

[6] E. Metzger, ed., *Law for All Times: Essays in Memory of David Daube* [*Roman Legal Tradition*, 2] (Lawrence, KS 2004).
[7] A. Rodger, 'Law for All Times: The Work and Contribution of David Daube', in E. Metzger, ed., *Law for All Times: Essays in Memory of David Daube* [*Roman Legal Tradition*, 2] (Lawrence, KS 2004), 9.
[8] Edinburgh 1974.
[9] Id., 92.
[10] D. Daube, 'The Scales of Justice', *Juridical Review*, 63 (1951), 109.

language and style of texts, whether they be legal, biblical, rabbinical or literary.'[11] Exploring the text-analysis point in a range of contexts brought the lecture to a fascinating discussion of the use of 'we' and 'our' by justices of the U. S. Supreme Court in referring to past decisions and the fact that one would not find this usage in the opinions of British appellate courts. Observing that 'it is at this point, as indeed so often, that I would love to turn to David', Alan Rodger notes that Daube 'would have given a thousand reasons to explain these phenomena, all better than any we can devise, and in private, at least, he would have quickly shown the weaknesses in any explanations which we put forward.'[12]

These limited comments cannot do justice to an absorbing lecture about a remarkable man. But from an Aberdeen perspective Alan Rodger's very last point — that Daube contributed to a pioneering team — is especially interesting and must be quoted:

> [H]e was a member of a remarkable team, including Tom Smith and Hamish Gow, who were pioneers in the reform of legal education . . . . We are all the beneficiaries of the new system which these men helped to create. In cherishing the work of David Daube and drawing inspiration from it, you are drawing on the rich inheritance of this wonderful, ancient, University of Aberdeen.[13]

This legacy is, indeed, something for Aberdeen to live up to in a world in which, of course, present standing counts for far more than past excellence.

David Daube's three sons Jonathan, Ben, and Mike and grandson Matthew came to Aberdeen for the lecture and conference. After the colloquium Jonathan told me that the family had decided to offer to the University his father's papers and books. While I gratefully accepted and considered the matter an unquestionable benefit to the University, the formal position was that this was an offer for Aberdeen University to consider and accept or decline. A decision was taken that Ernest Metzger should be invited to inspect the

---

[11] Rodger (note 7), 11.
[12] Id., 18.
[13] Id., 20–21. Hamish Gow: J. J. (Hamish) Gow (1918–2009). See *Scots Law News* for 25 February 2010 at the website of the University of Edinburgh School of Law.

collection and to report; he carried out the inspection in June 2002. Most of the materials were held with the Robbins Collection at Berkeley with a small part kept by Jonathan Daube at his home in Connecticut. On 18 June 2002 Metzger produced a report on the 'Proposed Gift of the Daube Papers to the University of Aberdeen'. The report was distributed to Paul Beaumont (Head of School); David Carey Miller (Deputy Head of School); Jonathan Daube; Robin Evans-Jones (Professor of Jurisprudence) and Alan Rodger. The Metzger Report arrived at the general assessment that: 'This is indeed a wonderful collection of materials, of lasting importance to scholars.'

Reduced to 23 large boxes for shipping purposes, the materials arrived in Aberdeen on 8 June 2005. A team led by Siobhan Convery, University Archivist and Head of Special Libraries and Archives, did excellent work in making the collection available for access by scholars. One can only look forward to future use of the material in what promises to be the outstanding space of a new library, presently under construction, very much the project of past Principal Sir Duncan Rice, who is mentioned later in this piece.

Professor Reuven Yaron, having learned of the donation of his mentor's papers, informed Ernest Metzger that he wished to gift to the University his Aberdeen correspondence and papers. This material, which is complementary to a sector of the Daube papers, arrived in Special Collections in May 2005. This most accomplished scholar, first member of the extraordinary group of brilliant talent making up the Daube pupils, contributed to the colloquium following the 2001 Aberdeen conference.[14] Professor Yaron, as senior figure, in his eighty-fifth year, was first speaker at the 2009 Centenary Conference. As he told, he first came to Aberdeen in 1954, having opted to work under Daube rather than Jolowicz at Oxford. In addition to the period from 1954 as Daube's pupil, Reuven Yaron taught at Aberdeen, first in session 1956/1957 soon after completing his doctorate under Daube at Oxford, and again in session 1965/1966 as Visiting Professor standing in

---

[14] R. Yaron, 'Remarks on Consensual Sale (with special attention to *periculum emptoris*)', in E. Metzger, ed., *Law for All Times* (note 6), 59.

for Peter Stein who was on sabbatical leave.

Sixty years before the David Daube centenary celebration, my Scottish postgraduate teacher, T. B. Smith, later Sir Thomas Smith, wrote in his inimitable style of Daube's standing and contribution. Commenting on the balance between the Civil law tradition and pressures from English common law influence in Scottish scholarship and legal education, Smith noted a positive development in the revival of pure Roman law studies and went on to say:

> This may in particular be associated with the name of Professor David Daube, formerly of the Chair of Jurisprudence at Aberdeen University and now Regius Professor of Civil Law at the University of Oxford. His successor at Aberdeen is one of his most brilliant pupils, and another occupies the Chair of Roman Law at Glasgow University. Yet a third proved himself an inspiring teacher at Aberdeen before accepting an appointment in the University of Jerusalem. These are all exponents of the pure Roman law in the greatest tradition. The 'Arbor Daubiana' stretches back over eight centuries of Civilian learning passed from master to disciple — from Irnerius in the twelfth century, through men such as Bulgarus, Azo, Accursius, Bartolus, Baldus, Donellus, Carpzovius, Heineccius and Lenel up to the present Regius Professor.[15]

Smith's confidence in Daube's brilliance and learning probably explains the latter's being consulted on the St Ninian's Isle treasure case when the University considered its position in terms of possible argument on appeal to the Inner House after losing before the Lord Ordinary.[16] But on this occasion there is no indication of a contribution from Daube, let alone a miracle argument, perhaps suggesting an astute assessment that taking on the *grundnorm* was a hopeless cause.

T. B. Smith's early 1960s list of Daube pupils can be brought up-to-date by reference to Alan Rodger's 2001 Aberdeen lecture referring to Daube's contribution at Oxford over the period 1955–1970.

---

[15] T. B. Smith, *Studies Critical and Comparative* (Edinburgh 1962), 62; first published as 'A Meditation on Scottish Universities and the Civil Law', *Tulane L. Rev.*, 33 (1959), 621. J. A. C. (Tony) Thomas was Douglas Professor of Civil Law at Glasgow from 1957 to 1964; he was taught by Daube at Cambridge in the late 1940s. Two of Daube's pupils were of course subsequent holders of the Douglas Chair: Alan Watson 1965–1968 and William Gordon 1969–1999.

[16] See D. L. Carey Miller, 'St Ninian's Isle Treasure: *Lord Advocate v University of Aberdeen and Budge*', in J. Grant and E. Sutherland, eds., *Scots Law Tales* (Dundee 2010), 126.

During his time in Oxford he was again an outstanding teacher, his lectures achieving something of a cult status. In addition, he gave leadership to a band of scholars who were interested in Roman law, including Barry Nicholas, Tony Honoré, Alan Watson, and a number of others. He also continued with his series of doctoral pupils which had begun earlier with Peter Stein: Reuven Yaron, Calum Carmichael, Alan Watson, Bernard Jackson and I all worked with him during this time.[17]

The idea of a centenary event came from David's son Jonathan, an Aberdeen arts graduate who had active contact with the University through his longstanding service as director of the North American alumni affairs programme. A very considerable volume of e-mail messages passed between Jonathan and me in the build up to the conference over a two-year period. The decision to run it was taken in early 2007 when I returned to the University after a period of leave in Sri Lanka between retiring from my full-time post and taking up part-time re-engagement. I was happy to have the opportunity to continue in the event-organizing role I had developed and enjoyed prior to retirement.

The distinguished contributors to the 2009 David Daube Centenary Conference included: Professor Reuven Yaron, author of three pioneering 1960s books on ancient law, who in the 1950s moved with his pupil-master Daube from Aberdeen to Oxford; Professor William Gordon, Roman law scholar and author of the definitive modern text on Scottish land law, who was taught by Daube at Aberdeen in the 1950s; Professor Alan Watson, Romanist and famous 'legal transplants' scholar, a pupil of Daube's at Oxford; Professor Bernard Jackson, distinguished scholar of Jewish law and studies, also an Oxford pupil; Lord Rodger of Earlsferry, scholar of Roman Law and Law Lord — now Justice of the United Kingdom Supreme Court — also supervised by Daube at Oxford; Professor Calum Carmichael of Cornell, taught by Daube at Oxford, and most prolific in the field of Daube scholarship. Unfortunately, Peter Stein's health meant that he could not be present.

Professor William Gordon, in the preface of the recent *Edinburgh Studies in Law* selection of his papers volume,

---

[17] Rodger (note 7), 7–8.

sees Daube's influence as a primary factor in his decision to opt for academic work rather than legal practice.

> Without the inspiration and encouragement of David Daube, of whose advanced class in Roman law at Aberdeen I was for two years the sole undergraduate member, it is doubtful whether I would have taken up an academic career as I had during my LLB studies simultaneously enjoyed an old-style apprenticeship....[18]

My own contact with David Daube was minimal; but I was fortunate enough to meet him on two occasions. Soon after my appointment to a lectureship in Aberdeen in 1971 I obtained a C. B. Davidson grant for a research visit to California to work with Dave Meyers, a Berkeley graduate, who had been a fellow student in Edinburgh. I took the opportunity to arrange a visit to Berkeley to meet David Daube. The warm response I had received to my request to visit was matched by hospitality on the day; the distinguished senior scholar who I held in awe turned out to be a most kind and friendly man. Professor Reuven Yaron happened to be visiting Berkeley from Jerusalem at the time of my visit. After David had shown me the Robbins Collection we met Reuven for coffee. As we sat down together at a Berkeley café table in the sun our host spontaneously said 'Aha, the three Aberdonians!'

David Daube's sense of humour had already been brought to my attention in what may be an apocryphal Aberdeen University tale of his requisitioning a chaise-longue for his room in the Taylor Building soon after his appointment. This unusual request produced a polite inquiry note from the relevant university office asking why he needed this particular item of furniture. The story goes that David replied to the effect that the strain of giving three lectures a week on Roman law made it essential for him to be able to rest in his office! Apparently he got his chaise-longue although it was no longer in the room which I moved into as senior member of the Department of Jurisprudence on Geoffrey MacCormack's early retirement in the mid-1990s.

The second occasion on which I met David Daube was when he came to Aberdeen at the age of eighty-one, some

---

[18] W. M. Gordon, *Roman Law, Scots Law and Legal History* (Edinburgh 2007), vii.

forty years after his appointment to the Chair of Jurisprudence, to receive an honorary LLD degree. David's son Jonathan and his grandson Matthew were with him. A number of other universities — including Cambridge, Edinburgh and the Sorbonne — had already honoured David but Jonathan later told me that the Aberdeen honorary LLD meant as much to his father as any of the others. Geoffrey MacCormack, fourth Professor of Jurisprudence — himself recipient of an honorary LLD in 2009 — gave the laureation address on 5 July 1990. Crediting Daube's appointment to Principal (later Principal Sir Thomas) Taylor he said: 'Taylor wished to give the Faculty the breadth and academic strength of a law school in the established continental European tradition.' Taylor, a religious man noted for his high moral standards, may have also been impressed by Daube's credentials in Jewish and New Testament studies. In any event, as Geoffrey MacCormack observed, the appointment was a great success.

The benefits for Aberdeen were immediate. Students enjoyed his inimitable style of lecturing. The grace, wit and humour which characterised his lectures have never been forgotten by those who attended them .... The Law Faculty became accustomed to a stream of visits from some of the most distinguished lawyers, philosophers and theologians in Europe. Daube brought Aberdeen into the mainstream of European legal culture ....[19]

It is clearly correct that David Daube's position in the teaching of Roman law and in civilian scholarship is a pivotal one. While his tenure of the Chair of Jurisprudence was relatively short it established an approach to civil law studies which was continued by Peter Stein for some twelve years and so came to be entrenched.

While one would not urge this as a matter of legal causation, a very recent major contribution to civil law learning can be traced back to the outstanding pupil of an outstanding master who both left Aberdeen to take up Regius chairs. The recent contribution is Gero Dolezalek's *Scotland under jus commune* published by The Stair Society in 2010.[20] In the

---

[19] Geoffrey MacCormack's address is published in *Aberdeen University Review*, 54 (1991), 65.
[20] G. Dolezalek, *Scotland under jus commune: Census of Manuscripts of Legal Literature in Scotland, mainly between 1500 and 1660* [Publications of the Stair Society, 55–57] (Edinburgh 2010).

words of Professor Hector MacQueen, this three volume census of sixteenth- and seventeenth-century Scottish legal manuscripts is a product of 'great scholarship and enormous energy' which lays 'a fresh base . . . for future research on a crucially formative period in the history of Scots law.'[21] The Chair of Civil Law which Professor Dolezalek held from 2005 to 2009 was created by Principal Sir Duncan Rice in the post-Quincentenary era giving Aberdeen a second professorial post potentially relevant to civilian learning. The first incumbent (1999 to 2005), it should be noted, was the distinguished South African civil law scholar Cornelius van der Merwe who contributed to the 2001 conference.[22] But was there a Stein factor which could be seen as ultimately Daube influenced? In session 1960/1961 an MA student C. D. Rice won the Faculty of Advocates' Prize in Professor Stein's Roman law class. Duncan Rice's return as Principal in 1997 more or less coincided with a Law School Research Assessment Exercise success but one felt that the new chair in Civil Law owed more to the profound influence of Peter Stein's Roman law class than any idea of a reward for an academic rating success.

A portrait of David Daube in doctoral robes hangs in the corridor on the fourth floor of the Taylor Building. More or less opposite it is a photograph of Gail Prudenti, a 1970s law graduate who became a Justice of the New York State Supreme Court and received an honorary LLD in 2004. The photograph was taken at a reception and Justice Prudenti has a glass in her raised hand. A colleague — who, like me, has a Taylor Building fourth floor room — recently observed that the judge seemed to be toasting the learned professor on the opposite wall who was surely responding with a definite twinkle of the eye. I like this image of a continuing presence in addition to the obvious legacy of scholarship which, thanks to a powerful loyalty, is represented at Aberdeen in tangible form in the Daube collection.

---

[21] Id., 1:xi (Foreword).
[22] See C. van der Merwe, 'Nova Species', in E. Metzger, ed., *Law for All Times* (note 6), 96.

II

David Daube and T. B. Smith

Hector L. MacQueen*

T. B. Smith was Dean of Law and Chair of Scots Law at the University of Aberdeen when Daube arrived in 1951. This began a thirty-year friendship, continuing through Daube's appointments in Oxford and Berkeley, and Smith's appointments as Chair of Civil Law and later Chair of Scots Law at the University of Edinburgh. Signs of their friendship are among Smith's private papers: offprints sent by Daube to Smith, and letters from Daube to Smith and his wife. A catalogue of the offprints is given in Appendix 1. *A selection of letters from Daube is set out in* Appendix 2. *A letter from Smith to Daube, from a separate collection, is set out in* Appendix 3. *An address by Smith, expressing thanks to Daube on the occasion of the latter's Gifford Lectures at the University of Edinburgh in 1962, is set out in* Appendix 4. *A partial list of authors represented among Smith's collection of offprints is set out in* Appendix 5.

Tony Weir has drawn our attention to five friendships in the law, or 'relationships to which — to use a lawyer's expression — lawyers were parties'.[1] While he drew no general conclusions about lawyers' friendships, the relationships surveyed

---

* Professor of Private Law, University of Edinburgh. I am indebted to Calum Carmichael and Alan Rodger for much help in the preparation of this paper. I am also grateful to Lady Ann Smith and the Daube family for permission to reproduce the unpublished writings of David Daube and T. B. Smith contained in the appendices to this article, and to Sir Alan Peacock for much appreciated assistance in other respects.

[1] T. Weir, 'Friendships in the Law', *Tulane Civil Law Forum*, 6/7 (1991/92), 61 (quotation at 93).

Hector L. MacQueen, 'David Daube and T. B. Smith', in E. Metzger, ed., *David Daube: A Centenary Celebration* (Glasgow: Traditio Iuris Romani, 2010), 11–36. Copyright © 2010 by Hector L. MacQueen (content) and Ernest Metzger (typographical arrangement). All rights reserved. ROMANLEGALTRADITION.ORG

'were good and rich'.² They include some of the great names of law — Domat, Holmes, Savigny — but it is fair to say that most of the other lawyers discussed by Weir gained their fame outside, or beyond, their profession — Montaigne, La Boétie, Boswell, Jakob Grimm — while some of these lawyers had friends — Pascal, Dr Johnson, Harold Laski — whose links with law came through their friendships and intellectual interests rather than from professional or academic commitment. This article merely adds one friendship to the examples discussed by Weir, but differs from them in that the friends were both academic lawyers. Their relationship began when they were colleagues in the Faculty of Law at Aberdeen University between 1951 and 1955, and lasted for over thirty years, despite very different approaches to their subject and the very different directions of their post-Aberdeen careers.

The relationship between David Daube and T. B. Smith has not been much explored in the now quite numerous writings on the lives and works of the two men, although it is clear that Daube's 1951 appointment to the Chair of Jurisprudence at Aberdeen during Smith's time as Dean of Law there was a major development in the former's academic career.³ It was also clearly a significant moment in the project, inspired by Aberdeen Principal Sir Thomas Taylor and led by Smith from his appointment to the Chair of Scots Law in 1948, to create a law school of international standing in Aberdeen. Daube was already a scholar of international repute in his fields of Roman and ancient Jewish law; when

---

[2] Id., 93.
[3] There are biographies of both men in the *Oxford Dictionary of National Biography*. For recent work on T. B. Smith, see E. Reid and D. L. Carey Miller, eds., *A Mixed Legal System in Transition: T B Smith and the Progress of Scots Law* (Edinburgh 2005); note also K. G. C. Reid, 'The Idea of Mixed Legal Systems', *Tulane Law Review*, 78 (2003), 5. For Daube, see A. Rodger, 'David Daube (8.2.1909–24.2.1999)', *Zeitschrift der Savigny-Stiftung für Rechtsgeschichte* (rom. Abt.), 118 (2001), xiv-lii; 'David Daube (1909-1999)', in J. Beatson and R. Zimmermann, eds., *Jurists Uprooted: German-speaking Émigré Lawyers in Twentieth-century Britain* (Oxford 2004), 233–48; and 'Law for All Times: the Work and Contribution of David Daube', *Roman Legal Tradition*, 2 (2004), 3. See also P. Stein, 'David Daube, 1909–1999', *Proceedings of the British Academy*, 111 (2000), 429; C. Carmichael, *Ideas and the Man: Remembering David Daube* (Frankfurt am Main 2004).

he departed from Aberdeen in 1955, it was to take up the Regius Chair of Civil Law at the University of Oxford, and he would go on from there in 1970 to become Director of the Robbins Hebraic and Roman Law Collections and Professor in the law school at Berkeley in California. The development of Smith's own international reputation had by contrast scarcely begun in 1951; but subsequently visiting appointments at Tulane (1957), Cape Town and Witwatersrand (both 1958) preceded his appointments to, first, the Chair of Civil Law at Edinburgh in 1958 and, second, to the Chair of Scots Law there in 1968. He became a full-time member of the Scottish Law Commission in 1972, holding that appointment until retirement in 1980. Smith was knighted in 1981 for his services to Scots law; his final project was the general editorship of the multi-volume *Laws of Scotland: Stair Memorial Encyclopaedia*. Smith died in 1988. Far away on the western seaboard of the USA, Daube became 'the world's oldest hippie'[4] and outlived Smith for eleven years, but also remained academically active until very near the end.

In his obituary of Daube in the *Zeitschrift der Savigny-Stiftung für Rechtsgeschichte* Alan Rodger notes:[5]

Smith ... saw it as his mission to project a vision of Scots Law as essentially a Civilian system of law which had come under too much influence from English law. Daube and he got on well together, even though they were very different men and Daube liked to poke fun at Smith's somewhat military bearing and outlook (Smith was a colonel). While Smith had no detailed knowledge of, or indeed interest in, classical Roman Law, he was favourably disposed towards the study of Roman Law in general. This proved useful when de Zulueta offered his Roman Law library to Aberdeen University for the token sum of £300 plus the cost of carriage. At the time Smith was active in developing the law library and, with his support, the University accepted de Zulueta's offer and so secured a substantial specialist library which provided Daube with the necessary materials for his work in Roman Law.

In his *Ideas and the Man: Remembering David Daube*, Calum Carmichael summarises these remarks by Rodger and adds in a footnote:[6]

---

[4] Carmichael, *Ideas and the Man* (note 3), 130.
[5] Rodger 2001 (note 3), xxvii. For de Zulueta see below notes 19 to 23 and accompanying text.
[6] Carmichael, *Ideas and the Man* (note 3), 94 n.4. Lady Ann Smith tells me that in fact T. B. Smith wore a kilt every day he could in Scotland (for example, to go for a walk or to formal dinners), but not when he went to

At my first meeting with Daube in Edinburgh in 1962, Daube introduced me to Smith [*who by this time held the Chair of Civil Law at Edinburgh University*]. After Smith left, Daube told me that, in Scotland, Smith never wore a kilt but did so every time he went to London. He wanted to remind those whom he met south of the Scottish border that London 'was not the centre of the United Kingdom, and certainly not the centre of the world.'

It is now possible to add a little flesh to these indicators that a friendship existed between Daube and Smith as a result of their shared Aberdeen years. Late in 2007 I was fortunate enough to come into possession of a quantity of Smith's private papers. Mostly these relate to the years he spent as a Scottish Law Commissioner between 1965 and 1980. But there is also a large collection of offprints, neatly organised into folders each bearing the name of the author whose works are gathered together within. The collection is clearly incomplete, since it includes only those whose surnames began with A, B, C and D. One of the bulkiest of these folders bears the name Daube, and inside there are some 40 offprints and photocopies of various Daube publications. A list may be found in Appendix 1. The majority of these prints are inscribed by Daube, and they range in date from 1948 to 1984. This suggests that their relationship endured until Smith's death in 1988. The inscriptions begin in a formal way — 'With the writer's compliments' — but soon move to what becomes the typical 'Kindest regards, David'. By the late 1970s, the regards had become 'warmest' or 'affectionate'.

But the evidence for enduring friendship contained within the offprint collection goes further than this. In amongst the offprints are three letters from Daube to Smith: the earliest antedating Daube's arrival in Aberdeen, as it is dated from Cambridge on 10 August 1950. The other two come from Daube's Berkeley days, being dated 2 April 1975 and 3 January 1985. Transcriptions may be found in Appendix 2. They confirm the affection in which Daube held, not only Smith, but his wife Ann. The later two letters are both addressed to the Smiths as a couple. The earliest of the letters makes it seem also probable that Ann Smith was significantly involved

work at the University (and not, in my personal observation, at the Scottish Law Commission either).

in making the Daube family welcome and at home in Aberdeen, and that this began even before the family's arrival, which probably took place in January 1951.

The letter of August 1950 suggests that Daube and the Smiths had already been communicating for some time in connection with the former's move from Cambridge to Aberdeen. The appointment must have been made earlier in the summer and no doubt as Dean of the Aberdeen Law Faculty Smith was responsible for ensuring as smooth a transition as possible for his new professor. Daube was replying to a letter from Smith received only after the former had returned from three weeks' holiday in France. They had evidently been interacting about where the Daubes were to live in Aberdeen, an important matter which had not been progressing as easily as might have been wished. No doubt Ann Smith had been involved here; and her hand may perhaps be detected also in the sending of presents to the Daube children. There was too a book for the parents, telling them something of the country where they would soon be living. This may have been a rather handsome volume. The book was most likely *Highways and Byways in the Central Highlands* by Seton Gordon (1886–1977), which was published in 1949 and for which Sir David Young Cameron (1865–1945), a very well-known painter-etcher, famous in particular for his etchings and drypoints of Highland Scotland, had provided the illustrations.[7]

Daube's reciprocation was an offprint on Hadrian's rescript to some ex-praetors, but this too was related to previous interaction with Smith, a discussion about the lapsing of the office of King's Counsel on the death of the king. Daube mentions in the article how practice changed in England from 1604, when King James I, induced by Francis Bacon, began to grant the office of King's Counsel so as to bind his successors. One can readily imagine Smith's interest in this, not only as

---

[7] On Gordon and Cameron see respectively Tom Weir, 'Gordon, Seton Paul (1886–1977)', *Oxford Dictionary of National Biography* (Oxford 2004), and W. N. Smith, 'Cameron, Sir David Young (1865–1945)', *Oxford Dictionary of National Biography* (Oxford 2004).

an advocate but also as a result of James having been king of Scots before succeeding to the English Crown in 1603.

The offprint which accompanied this letter may not have been the first which Smith had received from Daube. The earliest publication date of the offprints in the Smith collection is 1948; but there was most probably no link between the two men as early as that. The Hadrian's rescript offprint has the number 10 inscribed upon it, and sixteen others in the collection also have a numerical inscription ranging from 3 to 20 (the missing numbers are 1, 2 and 16).[8] The 1948 publication is actually numbered 20, and the overall numbering is certainly not in chronological order. But the bulk of the collection belongs to 1950 and 1951, although the latest — Numbers 14 and 15 — are from 1954 and 1955 respectively. An initial thought was that perhaps these numbered offprints were a collection made available to colleagues in Aberdeen at the time when Daube's name was under consideration for appointment to the Jurisprudence Chair. But while such a procedure may well have taken place and formed the starting point for Smith's collection, the numbering seems most likely to reflect a first attempt to organise it in the mid-1950s; and the attempt was not continued beyond its accomplishment at that point. There may be a link with Daube's departure from Aberdeen in 1955. Chronologically the last numbered publication was Daube's Oxford inaugural in February 1956. It is not inscribed by Daube, so possibly Smith picked it up of his own initiative, as an Oxford graduate as well as an interested colleague.

The occasions of the two remaining letters are more in the nature of Daube sharing jokes with the Smiths. The 1975 letter, which evidently came not long after the Smiths had visited Daube at Berkeley and seems not to have covered any

---

[8] See the list in Appendix 1. One wonders if the missing offprints included Daube's Aberdeen inaugural, 'The Scales of Justice', *Juridical Review*, 63 (1951), 105, and 'The Date of *The Birth of Merlin*', *Aberdeen University Review*, 35 (1953), 49. The latter might have been of interest because in it Daube found support for dating the play *The Birth of Merlin* in the reign of James I by noting how a pun on the name Britain may allude to events in 1604 when James I was proclaimed 'King of Great Britain, France and Ireland'. I owe this suggestion to Calum Carmichael.

offprint,[9] narrates the discovery by Berkeley researchers on the history of canon law that there had been a native-born Scottish saint in the middle ages, namely St Gilbert of Moray (d. 1243/5).[10] Stephan Küttner, to whom the letter refers, was Director of the Robbins Collection in Roman and Canon Law at Berkeley, holding that post from 1970 to 1988. The letter contains a typical Daube versification on the discovery of the saint, quoted in full for the benefit of the Smiths. The 'Somerville' who responded to Daube with a Latin verse of his own was Robert Somerville, a student of Küttner's who in 1982 would publish *Scotia Pontifica: Papal Letters to Scotland before the Pontificate of Innocent III*.[11] The 1985 letter accompanied an offprint of a *jeu d'esprit* on Shakespeare and Shakespeare's German translator, August Wilhelm Schlegel (1767–1845), and expressed the hope that 'you both will enjoy the joke about Shakespeare and that you, Tom, may find the condictio piece of some interest.' The second reference is to another, longer, 1984 article in the offprint collection, 'A corrupt judge sets the pace', from the *Gedächtnisschrift für Wolfgang Kunkel*, which includes a long discussion of the development of the *condictio*.

My limited knowledge of Daube's work does not allow me to say whether he chose to send Smith papers likely to be of especial interest to him. They are mostly on Roman law rather than other areas of Daube's specialisms, although there are also pieces on general topics such as genetics, procreation, marriage and suicide. Although there is little or no evidence on the prints of a reader's close scrutiny, such as side-scoring, underlining and marginalia, we certainly should not assume that Smith simply collected the offprints and left them unexamined. He was a man of wide interests and culture, educated in the classics and the Bible like all men of his generation and class; and amongst his other offprint correspondents were the classicists Maurice Bowra and Ken-

---

[9] It did however include photocopies of material about St Gilbert of Moray, the subject of the letter.
[10] See further on Gilbert, B. E. Crawford, 'Gilbert of Moray (d. 1243/5)', *Oxford Dictionary of National Biography* (Oxford 2004).
[11] R. Somerville, *Scotia Pontifica: Papal Letters to Scotland before the Pontificate of Innocent III* (Oxford 1982).

neth Dover. One therefore can readily imagine that Smith found something of interest in all the material he received from Daube. Perhaps the papers on delict, defamation, interpretation and medico-legal issues would have received the most attention for the purposes of his own scholarship. But unless we can find responses by Smith in the collection of Daube's correspondence now held in Aberdeen, or citations in Smith's own publications, we will never know for sure what his reactions to and uses of the these pieces may have been.[12]

We do know, however, that Smith reacted enthusiastically in December 1963 to another gift from Daube, a copy of *The Exodus Pattern in the Bible*, the book of the Gifford Lectures given in Edinburgh University in 1962.[13] The letter printed as Appendix 3 survives amongst Calum Carmichael's collection of Daube papers; the book may still exist in Smith's library.[14] Also published as Appendix 4 to this paper is the vote of thanks Smith gave at the conclusion of the delivery of these Gifford Lectures, on 11 October 1962. Smith was by this time firmly established in the Chair of Civil Law at Edinburgh, to which he had moved from Aberdeen in 1958. We can see that the tribute to Daube's 'remarkable gift of vision' was not simply the formal phraseology of one carrying out a necessary but essentially impersonal and official duty, but words drawing upon a friendship and collegiality of more than ten years' standing. It was probably also Smith who promoted the award of an honorary Edinburgh LLD to Daube

---

[12] Daube's 1951 article, '"Ne Quid Infamandi Causa": The Roman Law of Defamation', in *Atti del Congresso Internazionale di Diritto Romano e di Storia del Diritto* (Milan 1951), 413, which is in the offprint collection, is (mis-)cited in Smith's inaugural lecture at Edinburgh: 'Strange Gods: the Crisis of Scots Law as a Civilian System', *Juridical Review*, 71 (1959), 129 n.33 (reprinted in Smith's *Studies Critical and Comparative* (Edinburgh 1962), 79 n.33).

[13] The book was published in London by Faber in 1963.

[14] I believe that at least part of T. B. Smith's library was donated or bequeathed to the Law Society of Scotland, and the volumes are still to be seen around the Society's premises at 26 Drumsheugh Gardens, Edinburgh.

in 1960, the first such degree that the latter had received and one of which he was accordingly particularly proud.[15]

There is at least one piece of evidence in the offprint collection that Daube had read something by Smith: a reference in a 1967 publication to '2 *Scotland: the development of its laws and constitution* 732f (The British Commonwealth), (Keeton ed. 1962)'. This was one of Smith's books, published originally in 1955 and a precursor of his most famous work, *A Short Commentary on the Laws of Scotland*, also published in 1962. Daube's reference supports this sentence: 'Professor T. B. Smith, for Scots Law, favours the retention of the doctrine – prevalent in several states of the U.S.A. – that wanton publication of an old scandal is actionable irrespective of truth.'[16] Daube's inscription on the offprint drew Smith's attention to the citation.

The passage of gifts was not all one-way. We have already referred to the Smiths giving presents to the Daube family before their arrival in Aberdeen. There survives in the Daube library now held in Aberdeen University a copy of Sir John Skene's 1609 Scots language edition of medieval law texts entitled *Regiam Majestatem*, and inside is a card inscribed 'To Hansel the Chair. Ann and Tom.'[17] This was clearly a gift from the Smiths made on the occasion of Daube's inaugural lecture, 'The Scales of Justice', delivered on 30 April 1951.

Nothing in any of this serves to modify our understanding of either Daube or Smith. It merely amplifies the already known: that the two men got on well, and sustained a friendship over nearly 40 years, despite physical divides which grew greater with time, and differences in personality, temperament and scholarly approaches which were also considerable. The friendship was based on mutual sympathy, generosity

---

[15] Information from Jonathan Daube. The degree was awarded on 7 July 1960 (*University of Edinburgh Calendar 1960-1961*, ed. P. McIntyre (Edinburgh, 1960), 753)).

[16] 'The Marriage of Justinian and Theodora: Legal and Theological Reflections', *Catholic University of America Law Review*, 16 (1967), 380–99, at 383.

[17] The volume's title page bears two inscriptions as follows: (1) 'A Ker S & C'; (2) 'Ex libris Ricardi Powell senior Interior Templi armiger. Lex est mens quondam nulla perturbata affectu. Eadem est mens Regis et Legis'.

and humour rather than truly common intellectual interests. Daube's own comments in a collection of essays in honour of T B Smith, published in 1982, seem amply borne out:[18]

> To contribute to a volume in honour of T. B. Smith is a high privilege. Our association dates from the early fifties when I joined the Aberdeen Law Faculty under his energetic, purposeful and visionary Deanship. But he did not give only as a scholar. The home of Tom, Ann and their three children still lives on in my memory as a source of inspiration: the five of them were very distinct, differently endowed individuals, yet together they formed a wonderful family. I am deeply grateful for those years and the continued friendship since. If the following note is rather esoteric, Tom and Ann have such wide interests, both academic and in the world of affairs, that it is bound to touch on some of them.

Another possible initial bond between the two men was Francis de Zulueta, Regius Professor of Civil Law when Smith was a student at Oxford in the 1930s.[19] Smith dedicated a 1959 article, 'Meditation on Scottish Universities and the Civil Law', to Zulueta's memory after his death in 1958, and wrote there of his 'memories, regrets, gratitude and hope'.[20] The esteem in which Daube also held Zulueta is highlighted by both Rodger and Carmichael.[21] The two first met in Oxford in the 1930s, when Daube discovered that Zulueta's Spanish origins led him to sympathise with Franco's brand of fascism; but some anti-Semitic attitudes did not prevent him rendering much support to Jewish refugees from Nazi Germany and, subsequently, to Polish exiles as well.[22] Later, Daube believed that Zulueta had recommended his name to the Prime Minister to fill the Oxford chair in 1955. After Zulueta's death, Daube edited a memorial volume, *Studies in*

---

[18] 'Ahab and Benhadad: a municipal directive in international relations', *Juridical Review*, (1982), 62.

[19] On Zulueta see F. H. Lawson, 'Zulueta, Francis de (1878–1958)', *Oxford Dictionary of National Biography* (Oxford 2004). See also Lawson's *The Oxford Law School 1850-1965* (Oxford 1968), 108, 125. According to the *ODNB*, Zulueta's father was of Scottish descent in the female line from Brodie M'Ghie Willcox, one of the founders of the P. & O. Steam Navigation Company.

[20] *Tulane Law Review*, 33 (1959), 621 (= *Studies Critical and Comparative* (Edinburgh 1962), 62–71).

[21] Rodger 2001 (note 3), xxvii; Carmichael (note 3), 95–96.

[22] See C. Carmichael, *The Jottings of David Daube: Reflections from the Twentieth Century by One of its Foremost Legal Minds* (New York 2007), No. 50.

the Roman Law of Sale, published in 1959.²³ The arrival of Zulueta's library in Aberdeen in 1952, and the award to him of an honorary LLD of the university in 1953, therefore may well have been something of a joint operation which cemented the mutual goodwill of Daube and Smith.

At the conference where this paper was delivered, Professor Alan Watson expressed doubt as to the extent of Daube's goodwill for Smith. Professor Watson explained that when he was appointed to succeed Smith in the Edinburgh Chair of Civil Law in 1968, Daube warned him against Smith, on the grounds that he would try to interfere in the way Watson carried out the tasks of the appointment. Watson and Smith did indeed have a bad relationship at Edinburgh; it may be added that earlier Smith had also had bad relations with another Edinburgh professorial colleague, J. D. B. Mitchell. But this need not mean that Daube's warm professions of friendship for Smith over more than thirty years were insincere or hid what was actually dislike. Friends often have a more acute (and sympathetic) appreciation of each other's weaknesses than would their respective enemies; and it is possible to 'warn' one friend about aspects of another friend's character without intending thereby to deny the latter friendship. As a good friend of both Smith and Watson, Daube may well have sought to avert the probability of a clash of personalities when the two came together in Edinburgh; but if so, he was unsuccessful on this occasion.

I have a sense that Daube may have been more important for Smith's academic development than the other way round, significant for Daube though the Aberdeen chair opportunity certainly was. Smith's university career was still in its infancy when he met Daube, and contact with the much longer-established scholar must have had some influence in shaping Smith's ambition and sense of the possible in academic life. Here was a man who was publishing more in Italy, France and Germany than in the United Kingdom, across a huge range of subjects and, indeed, disciplines. In a number of

---

²³ Probably because the volume was a collection of specialist studies in classical Roman law, there was no contribution to it by T. B. Smith.

publications Alan Rodger has argued for the significance of Daube's example, not only in the development of Roman law studies in Britain after the Second World War, but in the raising of standards generally in British academic law in that period.[24] T. B. Smith was to be the standard-bearer in this regard in Scotland,[25] and perhaps we should see Daube as the exemplar which Smith had most immediately before him in those formative years at Aberdeen when he developed his credo and the mission upon which that set him for the rest of his career.

---

[24] See the works cited in note 3; see also P. Birks, 'Roman Law in Twentieth-Century Britain', in J. Beatson and R. Zimmermann, eds., *Jurists Uprooted: German-speaking Émigré Lawyers in Twentieth-Century Britain* (Oxford 2004), 249–68.
[25] See works referred to in note 3.

Appendix 1

Offprints etc. sent to T. B. Smith by David Daube

	Publication in chronological order of publication	Inscription (with TBS's numbering)
1.	On the use of the term *damnum*. 1948. Studi in onore di Siro Solazzi. Naples.	'Kindest regards, David'. *Autographed TB Smith*. (20)
2.	Hadrian's rescript to some ex-praetors. 1950. Zeitschrift der Savigny-Stiftung für Rechtsgeschichte (rom. Abt.), 67. Pp. 511–18.	'Kindest regards, DD'. *Accompanies letter of **10** August **1950**.* (10)
3.	Actions between *paterfamilias* and *filiusfamilias* with *peculium castrense*. 1950. Studi in memoria di Emilio Albertario. Milan. Pp. 435–74.	'Kindest regards, David'. (19)
4.	Jesus and the Samaritan woman. 1950. Journal of Biblical Literature, 69(2). Pp. 137–47.	'Kindest regards, D.' (5)
5.	*Demolior* as a passive. 1950. Classical Quarterly, 44. Pp. 119–20.	'Kindest regards, D.' (8)
6.	Rabbinic methods of interpretation and Hellenistic rhetoric. 1949. Hebrew Union College Annual, 22. Pp. 239–64.	'Kindest regards, D.D.' (6)
7.	The peregrine praetor. 1951.	*No inscription*. (4)

	Journal of Roman Studies, 41. Pp. 66–70.	
8.	Concerning the classifications of interdicts. 1951. Revue Internationale des Droits de l'Antiquité, 6. Pp. 23–78.	'With the writer's compliments'. (7)
9.	Four types of question. 1951. Journal of Theological Studies, 2(1). Pp. 45–48.	*No inscription.* (3)
10.	Negligence in the early Talmudic law of contract (Peshi'ah). 1951. Festschrift Fritz Schulz. Weimar. Pp. 124–47.	*No inscription.* (17)
11.	'Ne quid infamandi causa fiat': the Roman law of defamation. 1951. Atti del Congresso Internazionale di Diritto Romano e di Storia del Diritto. Milan. Pp. 413–50.	'Kindest regards, David'. (18)
12.	The palingenesia of Digest 50.17.110 and the construction of asyndetons. 1952. Archives d'Histoire du Droit Oriental et Revue Internationale des Droits de l'Antiquité, 1. Pp. 385–99.	'Kindest regards, David'
13.	Generalisations in D. 18. 1, *de contrahenda emptione*. 1952. Studi in onore di Vincenzo Arangio Ruiz, 1. Naples. Pp. 185–200.	*No inscription.* (13)
14 .	Eisern vieh. 1952. Zeitschrift der Savigny-Stiftung für Rechtsgeschichte, romanistische	'With many thanks David'. (12)

Abteilung, 69. Pp. 388–92.

15 . Princeps legibus solutus. 1954. Studi in memoria di Paolo Koschaker. Milan. Pp. 463–65.   *No inscription.* (14)

16 . A meaning of 'cupiditas'. 1954. Studi in Onore di Pietro de Francisci, 1. Milan. Pp. 123–26.   'Kindest regards, D'. (9)

17 . Purchase of a prospective haul. 1955. Studi in onore di Ugo Enrico Paoli. Florence. Pp. 203–209.   'Kindest regards David'. (15)

18. The defence of superior orders in Roman law. 1956. An inaugural lecture delivered before the University of Oxford on 8 February 1956. Oxford.   *No inscription.* (11)

19 . Zur Palingenesie einiger Klassikerfragmente. 1959. Zeitschrift der Savigny-Stiftung für Rechtsgeschichte, romanistische Abteilung, 76. Pp. 149–264. [In German.]   'Kindest regards, David'

20 . Concessions to sinfulness in Jewish law. 1959. Journal of Jewish Studies, 10 (1 and 2). Pp. 1–13.   'Kindest regards, David'

21. Condition prevented from materializing. 1960. Tijdschrift voor Rechtsgeschiedenis, 28. Pp. 271–96.   'Kindest regards, David'

22 . Utiliter agere. 1960. Iura, 11. Pp. 69–148.   'Kindest regards, David'

23. Three notes having to do with Johanan Ben Zaccai. 1960. Journal of Theological Studies, 11(1). Pp. 53–62.

    'Kindest regards, David'

24. Texts and interpretation in Roman and Jewish law. 1961. The Jewish Journal of Sociology, 3(1). Pp. 3–28.

    'Greetings David'

25. To exact a debtor. 1961. Studi in onore di Emilio Betti, 2. Milan. Pp. 323–30.

    'Kindest regards, David'

26. D.19.1.46 and adultery. 1963. Mélanges Philippe Meylan, 1. Lausanne. Pp. 65–69.

    'Kind regards David'

27. The Lex Fufia Caninia and King Arthur. 1964. Law Quarterly Review, 80. Pp. 225–27.

    No inscription.

28. Dividing a child in antiquity. 1966. California Law Review, 54. Pp. 1630-37.

    'Greetings David'

29. The marriage of Justinian and Theodora: legal and theological reflections. 1967. Catholic University of America Law Review, 16(4). Pp. 380–99.

    'See footnote 18, David'.

30. The linguistics of suicide. 1972. Philosophy and Public Affairs, 1. Pp. 387–437.

    Photocopy missing several pages at the front. Complete from 402–437.

31. Withdrawal: five verbs. 1974. California Studies in Classical Antiquity, 7. Pp. 93–112.

    No inscription.

32. Medical and Genetic Ethics: 'Warmest regards
    Three Historical Vignettes.   David'
    1976. Oxford Centre for Post-
    graduate Hebrew Studies.

33. The Duty of Procreation. 1977.   'With affectionate
    Edinburgh.   regards, David'.
        Photocopy.

34. Counting. 1977. Mnemosyne,   *No inscription.*
    30. Pp. 176–78.

35. Historical aspects of informal   *No inscription.*
    marriage. 1978. Revue Interna-   *Photocopy.*
    tionale des Droits de l'Antiquité,
    25. Pp. 95–107.

36. 'Suffrage' and 'precedent',   *No inscription.*
    'mercy' and 'grace'. 1979.   *Photocopy, possibly*
    Tijdschrift voor Recht-   *of page proofs?*
    geschiedenis, 47. Pp. 235–46.

37. Fashions and idiosyncrasies in   *No inscription.*
    the exposition of the Roman law   *Typescript.*
    of property. 1979. Theories of
    Property. Ed. A. Parel and T.
    Flanagan. Waterloo, Ontario.

38. Greek forerunners of Simenon.   *No inscription.*
    1980. California Law Review,   *Photocopy.*
    68. Pp. 301–312.

39. Schlegel and Shakespeare.   *No inscription.*
    1984. Rechtshistorische   *Accompanies letter*
    Journal, 3. Pp. 183–86.   *of 3 January 1985.*

40. A corrupt judge sets the pace.   *No inscription.*
    1984. Gedächtnisschrift für   *Photocopy.*
    Wolfgang Kunkel. Ed. D. Nörr
    and D. Simon. Frankfurt am

Main. Pp. 37–52.

Numbered items (in numerical order)

1, 2. *Missing.*

3. Four types of question. 1951. Journal of Theological Studies, 2(1). Pp. 45–48.

4. The peregrine praetor. 1951. Journal of Roman Studies, 41. Pp. 66–70.

5. Jesus and the Samaritan woman. 1950. Journal of Biblical Literature, 69(2). Pp. 137–47.

6. Rabbinic methods of interpretation and Hellenistic rhetoric. 1949. Hebrew Union College Annual, 22. Pp. 239–64.

7. Concerning the classifications of interdicts. 1951. Revue Internationale des Droits de l'Antiquité, 6. Pp. 23–78.

8. *Demolior* as a passive. 1950. Classical Quarterly, 44. Pp. 119–20.

9. A meaning of 'cupiditas'. 1954. Studi in Onore di Pietro de Francisci, 1. Milan. Pp. 123–26.

10. Hadrian's rescript to some ex-praetors. 1950. Zeitschrift der Savigny-Stiftung für Rechtsgeschichte (rom. Abt.), 67. Pp. 511–18.

11. The defence of superior orders in Roman law. 1956. An inaugural lecture delivered before the University of Oxford on 8 February 1956. Oxford.

12. Eisern vieh. 1952. Zeitschrift der Savigny-Stiftung für Rechtsgeschichte, romanistische Abteilung, 69. Pp. 388–92.

13. Generalisations in D. 18. 1, *de contrahenda emptione*. 1952. Studi in onore di Vincenzo Arangio Ruiz, 1. Naples. Pp. 185–200.

14. Princeps legibus solutus. 1954. Studi in memoria di Paolo Koschaker. Milan. Pp. 463–65.

15. Purchase of a prospective haul. 1955. Studi in onore di Ugo Enrico Paoli. Florence. Pp. 203–209.

16. *Missing*.

17. Negligence in the early Talmudic law of contract (Peshicah). 1951. Festschrift Fritz Schulz, 1. Weimar. Pp. 124–47.

18. Ne quid infamandi causa fiat': the Roman law of defamation. 1951. Atti del Congresso Internazionale di Diritto Romano e di Storia del Diritto. Milan. Pp. 413–50.

19. Actions between *paterfamilias* and *filiusfamilias* with *peculium castrense*. 1950. Studi in memoria di Emilio Albertario. Milan. Pp. 435–74.

20. On the use of the term *damnum*. 1948. Studi in onore di Siro Solazzi. Naples.

Appendix 2

Letters to Tom (and Ann) Smith

1.

29 Chesterton Hall Crescent
Cambridge
10 August 1950[26]

My dear Smith

Yesterday we returned from France, and as our mail had not been forwarded, it was only then that your charming letter reached us. Of your much too generous presents to the children, Jonathan had indeed written to us in France. Do you know that we always wanted to buy the Story of Babar for Jonathan when he was small, but thought it too extravagant. Now an old wish is fulfilled. The ABC has all the French elegance. And the Central Highlands are a joy to read. I am looking forward to seeing the lovely places sketched by D. Y. Cameron.

We had a grand time in France, the Cathedrals of Coutances and Lamballe, the Mont St. Michel and the sleepy old town of Briquebec (an unexpected discovery, but sanctioned by Queen Victoria's approval) being the outstanding events. The weather was favourable throughout the three weeks. The only rainy day was when I was anyhow exceedingly lazy after too much *cidre*, the alcoholic qualities of which I had underestimated. But the peninsula from Cherbourg to Avranches has suffered terribly.

I need not repeat how much I appreciate your and your wife's patience and thoughtfulness regarding the problem of our house. I enclose a letter I am sending to Colonel Milne. You will see that I have taken your advice. But probably the

---

[26] This letter, unlike the other two printed here, is typed apart from the signature.

houses are sold already. I am sending Alec Parker another copy of the letter.

You may remember that I mentioned to you something about the office of King's Counsel lapsing or not lapsing on the king's death. You were kind enough to declare yourself interested. So would you glance at the last paragraph of the attached note, on p. 518.

I hope you are all enjoying your stay in Devon.

My wife asks to be remembered.

Kindest regards

Yours ever

David Daube

2.

From Berkeley
2 April 1975[27]

My dear Tom and Ann

This story from my library floor may amuse you. Apparently one of Kuttner's crew had challenged another to find a single real Scotsman — actually born in Scotland — in the calendar of saints. Well, the rara avis did emerge in the person of St Gilbert of Moray, Bishop of Caithness in the 13th century. I was informed of this yesterday morning and invited to attend a celebration — in the afternoon, since April 1 was his day (no April joke). Unfortunately I was already booked. But I did send the Canonists the following lines for the occasion:

When down in a trough,

---

[27] This letter has an enclosure of photocopied material on Gilbert from nineteenth-century publications.

cheer up, friends, and bless
the memory of
the star of Caithness.
He shows us how not
To doubt or be faint –
since even a Scot
can end up a saint.
He may be a Whig,
he may be a Tory:
let's all take a swig
to St Gilbert of Mory.[28]

As you may expect, today I received an elegant Latin note of thanks from my colleagues. [Note: Bob Somerville, to be precise: Tibi gratias ego, clarissime professor, de carmina tuo festivo Gilberto episcopo Cathinensi.]

I hope you will find your way back and stay much longer. You would discover a great deal to enjoy, on many levels.

Affectionate regards

David

3.

From Berkeley
3 January 1985

My very dear Friends

Thanks. Your generosity is inspiring and I am very, very grateful.

---

[28] St Gilbert is no longer the only native-born Scottish saint, following the canonisation of St John Ogilvie in 1976. Ogilvie is also the only post-Reformation Scottish saint (so far). Many locally venerated Scottish saints who may or may not have been born in the country are not recognised as such by the Roman Catholic Church.

I have been very sick, the emphysema having gotten much worse. But at the moment I am better, though reduced.

I hope you both will enjoy the joke about Shakespeare and that you, Tom, may find the condictio piece of some interest.

Love from

David

Appendix 3

Letter from T. B. Smith to David Daube

11 India Street
Edinburgh 3

27 Dec 63

My dear David

Congratulations and warmest thanks. *The Exodus Pattern in the Bible* has been a gift most highly valued, and I have read it with the greatest admiration and excitement. I knew that I could not come to this experience with the specialist background which a man such as Reuven[29] has, but you will not reject the less gifted recognition of one in the outer court that this book of yours is a masterpiece. It was Archie[30] who recalled the dictum that you had the gift of saying the obvious — but no one realised the obvious until you had said it. In a sense this is true of your theme for me. The association of ideas would never have occurred to me: now they seem most significant.

Our thoughts are v. much with you at the present time and we look forward eagerly to the second series of Gifford Lectures.

Our love and warmest greetings at New Year.

Aye yours

Tom

---

[29] Professor Reuven Yaron.
[30] Professor Archie Campbell of the Faculty of Law, Edinburgh University.

Appendix 4

T. B. Smith's Vote of Thanks to David Daube: Gifford Lectures, University of Edinburgh, 11 October 1962

Mr. Chairman, Ladies and Gentlemen, I rise with due diffidence because I remember that the Wise Men who choose appropriate Chairmen for these Lectures chose me as representative of Error and Ignorance. But if some of us in this room a fortnight ago in error and ignorance, we have gone through an attack of bad conscience, we have led to repentance, to confession, to self-judgment, and to a better understanding. We who are lawyers have long known Professor Daube for his learning and his brilliance as one of the greatest living scholars in Roman Law. During these Lectures we have learned much more of his extraordinary gifts, and his extraordinary learning in early law, in early thought, legal and religious, his scholarship in Hebrew and other languages, in his achievement in biblical Rabbinical scholarship, his quality in the study of Moral Philosophy and Theology. All this vast learning can be quite dry and quite fruitless in many men. With Professor Daube it is illumined and enlivened by the gift which he has shown in his writings, the gift of the fresh eye with which he looks at a problem and very often sees the solution which has escaped other people whose vision has been blinded by their learning, and, if he doesn't actually see the solution, he at least puts the problem into a new light which makes us see it in a new way, makes us think along new lines which will lead, one hopes, very soon to the solution. Now, his learning, this remarkable gift of vision he has applied in these Lectures to certain problems which are of fundamental importance to the theologian, to the philosopher and to the lawyer, problems of causation, problems of indent, negligence, problems of liability, liability for the completed act, a liability for the attempt, problems of interest to the psychologist, the reaction of the Doer after the act - on all of these he has enriched our knowledge and illumined our understanding - his Lectures have been a most memorable contribution to the history of human thought on certain

and very important subjects, and for this contribution, in your name, I offer him our most admiring and grateful thanks.

Thank you very much indeed.

Appendix 5

List of Authors in T. B. Smith's Offprint Collection

A	B	C	D
Sir C. K. Allen	B. Beinart	D. F. Cavers	J. Dainow
M. Ancel	J.M. Bemmelen	C. Carabiber	D. Daube
J. N. D. Anderson	Sir N. Birkett	M. Cappelletti	R. David
J. A. Ankum	L. Blom-Cooper	A. H. Campbell	J. P. Dawson
A. E. Anton	P. Q. R. Boberg	Lord Chalfont	R. W. M. Dias
A. L. Armitage	V. Bolgar	G. C. Cheshire	W. F. Dickson
D. I. C. Ashton-Cross	Sir M. Bowra	A. G. Chloros	W. C. Dickinson
L. W. Athulathmudali	G. W. S. Barrow	Sir G. Clark	Lord Diplock
P. S. Atiyah	R. S. Baver	E. M. Clive	J. Dixon
	A. W. Bradley	Lord Cohen	K. J. Dover
	Judge W. J. Brennan	M. Cohen	R. Dorat
	W. J. Brocklebank	H. Coing	
	A. W. Brown	J. C. Cooper	
	H. P. Brown	Lord Cooper[31]	
	L. Neville Brown	D. V. Cowen	
		M. Craffe	
		B. E. Crawford	
		P.-A. Crepeau	
		G. F. Curtis	

---

[31] In view of my previously published doubts as to the closeness of the relationship between Smith and Cooper (see my 'Two Toms and an Ideology for Scots Law: T B Smith and Lord Cooper of Culross', in E. Reid and D. L. Carey Miller, eds., *A Mixed Legal System in Transition: T B Smith and the Progress of Scots Law* (Edinburgh 2005), 44–74), note that Smith's collection consisted of three copies of Cooper's Saltire Society pamphlet of 1949, *The Scottish Legal Tradition* (but one of these the 1960 reprint, and none of them inscribed), and three other items, all inscribed 'TBS from TMC', viz., a copy of the 1950 issue of the *Harvard Law Review* containing Cooper's article, 'The Common Law and the Civil Law — a Scot's View'; the pamphlet publishing his 1952 David Murray Lecture, *The Dark Age of Scottish Legal History*; and an offprint of 'Defects in the British Judicial Machine', *Journal of the Society of Public Teachers of Law*, 2 (1952/54), 91–100, reprinted in his *Selected Papers 1922–1954* (Edinburgh and London, 1957), 244–58. Lady Ann Smith confirms that Smith had 'a close relationship with Lord Cooper, whom he revered greatly and who was very kind to him in his early years of "legal writing"' (personal communication, 19 July 2009).

III

David Daube on Causation in the Bible

Robert A. Segal*

This article analyses David Daube's defence of biblical law as sophisticated rather than 'primitive'. It focuses on the concept of causation. By 'primitive', Daube means, first, causation taken as exclusively direct. Biblical law, he argues, is not primitive because it recognises indirect as well as direct causation. By 'primitive', Daube means, second, causation taken as exclusively intentional. Biblical law, he argues, is not primitive because it recognises accidental as well as intentional causation. This article then argues that Daube's argument would have been enriched by a fuller consideration of the concept of 'primitive' itself. Examples from two celebrated anthropological authorities, E. B. Tylor and E. E. Evans-Pritchard, are discussed. By Tylor's characterization of 'primitive', Daube could have made an even stronger case that the biblical notion of causation is not primitive. By Evans-Pritchard's characterization of 'primitive', Daube would have had a harder time making his case.

David Daube argues for the conceptual sophistication of biblical thinking.[1] Sometimes he argues that biblical thinking is not 'primitive'. Other times he argues that not even pri-

---

* Sixth Century Professor of Religious Studies, School of Divinity, History and Philosophy, University of Aberdeen.
[1] D. Daube, 'Direct and Indirect Causation in Biblical Law', *Vetus Testamentum*, 11 (1961), 246–69, republished in C. Carmichael, ed., *Biblical Law and Literature* [*Collected Works of David Daube*, 3] (Berkeley 2003), 409–27.

mitive thinking is primitive. Let us assume the former: that biblical thinking is not primitive. For Daube, a primitive understanding of law would recognise only direct causation. Biblical thinking, he argues, recognises indirect as well as direct causation. Whenever biblical law does not hold anyone culpable for indirectly causing harm, the reason is not the inability of the Bible to grasp the notion of indirect cause but the difficulty of establishing culpability. The reason is legal, not conceptual.

Daube makes two sets of distinctions: on the one hand that between direct and indirect causes, on the other hand among the kinds of things that either directly or indirectly can serve as causes.

The distinction between direct and indirect causes is itself clear. To cite one of Daube's examples: 'The narrative of David and Uriah is old. No murder could be less direct, yet Nathan charges David: "Uriah the Hittite thou hast smitten with the sword."'[2] King David, having seen from his roof Uriah's wife, the beautiful Bathsheba, bathing, sends for her and has sex with her. He then calls her husband to his house, discloses nothing, and eventually entrusts him with a secret letter to Joab, David's general, in which David orders Joab to send Uriah to the front of the fiercest fighting and then to withdraw, leaving Uriah exposed and thereby certain to be killed. The tactic works. At the news of her husband's death, Bathsheba mourns. At the end of the period of mourning, David sends for her and marries her.

God then sends Nathan, the court prophet, to rebuke David. Nathan uses one of the most celebrated parables in the Hebrew Bible to do so. Unaware that the parable, which is presented as an actual event, is meant to apply to him, David immediately orders the punishment of the culprit. Nathan then informs David that he, David, is the culprit. David immediately acknowledges his guilt. The punishment that Nathan prophesies is ceaseless fighting within David's family, and it comes true. The son that Bathsheba has just borne David from their tryst is also to die. David himself is spared.

---

[2] Id., 246.

Subsequently, Bathsheba bears him a second son, Solomon, who is David's favourite (see 2 Samuel 11–12).[3]

This incident, like the various others from the Bible and elsewhere that Daube notes, assumes indirect causation. David did not have to be the one who killed Uriah still to be culpable for Uriah's death. Daube does not consider the possible legal culpability of Joab, whose sense of guilt seemingly had to be assuaged by a follow-up message from David. Daube certainly does not consider any legal culpability on the part of the Ammonite fighter or fighters who directly killed Uriah.

Daube is writing to 'expose the baselessness of any theory which would explain the rigidity of early statutes in the matter of causation by an inability to grasp a less obvious nexus.'[4] But then why does biblical law often give 'narrow definitions' of culpability — that is, confine itself to direct, easily determined causes? Daube's answer:

For practical, technical reasons, reasons of machinery; above all, because less direct causation usually does mean less certainty, and in an age without a highly organized police force, forensic laboratories, truth drugs and so on that uncertainty is prohibitive. The law cannot exact retribution where the evidence leaves a degree of doubt.[5]

Daube cites the difference between the beating to death of a slave by a master and the killing of one free man by another. In the case of the slave 'Vengeance is sanctioned only "if he [the slave] die under his hand", and is expressly excluded "if he [the slave] continue a day or two".'[6] By contrast, there is no time limit imposed in the case of the free man. The reason for the difference is that 'A master may [lawfully] beat his slave constantly. If vengeance were lawful even should death occur after weeks or months, he [the master] would be in danger whenever a slave of his died. [For i]t could always be connected with a beating.'[7] By contrast, 'Two free men will not normally fight every day, an injury is an

---

[3] By contrast, 1 Sam 13:14 glosses over David's sin with Bathsheba, and 1 Chron 20:1–3 omits it altogether.
[4] Daube (note 1), 247.
[5] Id., 247–48.
[6] Id., 248.
[7] Id., 248–49.

isolated occurrence, [and] its development for better or worse can be watched' to see whether it leads to the injured man's death.[8] If the same rule applied to the beating of a slave, beating per se would become illegal since any eventual death could be attributed to a beating. In the case of a free man who is injured by another and 'must take to his bed', there is a time limit set: 'It is laid down that "if he [the injured] rise again and walk abroad upon his staff, then shall he that smote him be quit" [i.e., be acquitted].'[9] Once the injured free man becomes ambulatory, then any subsequent injury [or just death?] gets blamed on a subsequent cause.

If by 'primitive' Daube means the restriction of causation to direct causation, he also means the restriction of causation to intent: 'It is sometimes maintained that in primitive law, either you have caused death with intent or, if not, you are regarded as not having caused it at all: some other cause must be considered exclusively responsible.'[10] Daube demurs. Just as for him biblical law allows for indirect causation, so for him it allows for accidental causation. Daube cites a case of accidental homicide:

> ... the two men hewing wood together and one unwittingly killing the other. He does not do it with his hands, he does not even do it by a direct blow with the axe; but as he swings down the axe, the iron head flies from the handle and the other man is hit.[11]

The person who accidentally commits the killing is still guilty, just less guilty than he would have been if the killing had been intentional.[12]

As further evidence of the sophistication of biblical law, Daube cites a distinction made within accidental harm: the difference between someone's lighting a fire on his own land that then unintentionally spreads to a neighbour's land,

---

[8] Id., 249.
[9] Id., 248.
[10] Id., 253.
[11] Id., 252 (on Deut 19:5).
[12] This case is meant to illustrate the need for the establishment of cities of refuge in the Promised Land to enable the 'killer' to avoid being pursued by a blood relative. If none of the three cities was sufficiently close, the relative might 'pursue and overtake and put the killer to death, although a death sentence was not deserved, since the two had not been at enmity before.' Deut 19:6.

thereby causing damage to property, and the coming off of the head of the axe, thereby causing death. In the case of the fire there is 'full civil law liability despite the indirectness'. In the case of the axe there is 'mitigated criminal law liability' because 'there is no intent'.[13]

Daube draws a link between accidental harm and indirect causation. While, as noted, intentional harm can be inflicted indirectly, accidental harm is invariably indirect: 'Accidental homicide does normally involve some indirectness; and in the specimen case under review, with the head of the axe coming off, the indirectness is of such a nature as to furnish practically conclusive evidence of absence of intent.'[14]

In the case of the axe, Daube introduces several possible causes beyond that of the person who swung the axe: 'if a disaster results from the head of an axe flying off, the person who swung the axe is a cause in one sense at least, namely, as having triggered off the chain of events, though in another sense, as a thinking being, he is not, so that from this angle prominence must be accorded to the axe or to fate or to God.'[15] What is the exact status of (a) the axe, (b) fate, and (c) God?

(a) The axe. Daube writes that 'Biblical law knows no proceedings against an inanimate killer.'[16] He does note 'tendencies which might have led to such proceedings: an ox that kills a man is to be stoned'[17] — a notion akin to the famous medieval trial of a pig. But he then writes that 'it would be arbitrary, [just] for the sake of what some moderns

---

[13] Daube (note 1), 253. As yet further evidence of the sophistication of biblical law, Daube cites another distinction made within indirect causation: the difference between on the one hand a man's digging a pit into which another man's animal falls or a man's ox killing another man's ox and on the other hand a man's cattle pasturing in another man's field or, as noted, fire spreading from one man's land to another (see Exod 21:33–36; 22:4–6). In the first two cases 'the chief basis of liability ... is ownership of the object causing the damage': the pit and the ox. The owner has failed to cover the pit and failed to guard the ox. In the second two cases the owner is liable not because something belonging to him causes damage but because he 'set[s] the agent to work' — by 'letting go' of the cattle and by letting out of the fire. Daube (note 1), 259.

[14] Daube (note 1), 253.
[15] Id.
[16] Id., 254.
[17] Id.

feel primitives ought to have felt, to postulate such an institution.'[18] So presumably Daube is rejecting the view that primitives held culpable inanimate entities, even if they did hold animals culpable. Here, as elsewhere, Daube shifts the issue — from whether the Bible is primitive to whether what is called primitive is primitive. Again, I will stick to the former.

(b) Fate. Daube does not discuss.

(c) God. Daube writes that

> In the same ancient code which contains the statute about fire, accidental homicide appears as the case where 'he lie not in wait but God let it happen to his hand'. We have not enough detail to say precisely what kind of situation is contemplated: even here, in all probability, not primarily a blow with the hand but, for example, the throwing of an object which unexpectedly hits somebody.[19]

How literally is the role of God meant? Daube writes that

> the Biblical statute, by ascribing the event to God who uses the person's hand, not only introduces a profound theological concept but also greatly advances a unified view of all accident: the manifold visible agents — hand, axe, stone — are equally directed by the ultimate mover and, indeed, the case is fundamentally equated with accident in which no human cause is discerned at all.[20]

Daube objects, in by-now litany-like fashion, to the conclusion that the biblical view is primitive because 'causation and intent ... are invariably combined' — which here would mean the assumption that the hand or the axe or the axe head is considered to be the willful agent.[21]

But then what for Daube is the role of God? If on the one hand he vigorously denies that the Bible is incapable of conceiving of accidental causation, on the other hand he is asserting that in this example God is deliberately causing the implement to hit the victim. Indeed, while he grants that 'No doubt the limbs and organs of a person were often thought of as, up to a point, forces in their own right', 'it is up to a point only'.[22] He is reluctant to 'animate' inanimate objects. But if

---

[18] Id.
[19] Id., 254–55.
[20] Id., 255.
[21] Id.
[22] Id.

the hand is not the instigator here, God must be. But that option raises questions that at least here Daube does not consider: when does God intervene and in what way? The Bible is, of course, full of examples of events in which God plays a causal role, but exactly what that role is often varies. Against the claim that the hand is here deemed the willful perpetrator, Daube notes the case of a woman's hand being cut off — but only 'for a despicable outrage'.[23] In other words, the cutting off of the hand is meant to punish the woman and not, as if a separate entity, her hand (see Deuteronomy 25:11–12).

Daube's paper would have been abetted by a fuller consideration of 'primitive'. Let me note two classical characterizations. There are many other possible characterizations, and I am noting these two simply as examples.

In *Primitive Culture*[24] the pioneering anthropologist Tylor, while not coining the term 'animism', popularizes it. For him, animism means religion per se, not merely primitive religion. Animism is the belief in souls in all things. In its earliest, primitive phase, animism means the existence of souls in things that for moderns are *inanimate*: 'stocks [sticks?] and stones, weapons, boats, food, clothes, ornaments, and other objects which to us are not merely soulless but lifeless.'[25] For Tylor, a soul gives life — animation — to a body, so that soulless means lifeless. Initially, the soul is believed to reside within the body. Subsequently, the soul is believed to reside outside the body but still to control it. Initially, each entity — for example, each stone — has its own soul. Eventually, there is just one soul for all stones. Ultimately, there is a single god controlling all things, and from outside. In the primitive stage of animism not only inanimate objects but also all animate ones have souls, likewise first one per object and one residing within the object, then eventually one per species and one residing outside the objects. Thus plants and animals also all have souls. Human beings too have souls. The souls of all entities except for humans are gods, for which

---

[23] Id.
[24] E. B. Tylor, *Primitive Culture: Researches into the Development of Mythology, Philosophy, Religion, Art, and Custom*, 1st ed. (London 1871).
[25] Id., 2:61.

Tylor prefers the term 'spirits'. Gods are nothing more than the souls of all entities apart from humans.

For Tylor, religion is the primitive counterpart to science, which is exclusively modern. Where religion attributes every event in the physical world to a decision by a god or a human being, science attributes every event in the physical world to an impersonal process. In religion, fire spreads intentionally — the effect of a decision by the god of the specific fire at hand or by the god of fire per se or by the sole god of everything. In science, fire spreads for chemical reasons. Religion and science are mutually exclusive.[26]

The link to law is that for Tylor the heart of animation is motion and deliberate motion. All motion — all behaviour — is intentional and also direct. Even if in later stages of animism a god of everything decides to spread a fire, the god acts directly and not through something else. In the primitive phase of animism a stone over which one trips has placed itself there so that one will trip over it: 'what we call inanimate objects — [individual] rivers, stones, trees, weapons, and so forth — are treated as living intelligent beings, talked to, propitiated, *punished for the harm they do*.'[27] Parts of the body are likewise considered autonomous animate beings. By Tylor's conception of 'primitive', harm is therefore always both intentional and direct. The hand, the axe, or the axe head — I do not know how one would decide which — would be an animate entity that decided to kill the victim. Culpability would rest with the hand, the axe, or the axe head, not with the person whose hand, axe, and axe head it was. Nor would

---

[26] To be sure, Tylor allows for the continuation of religion in modern times, but only in a reduced role, and a role severed from the physical world.

[27] Tylor (note 24), 2:61 (emphasis added). In the fashion of his day, Tylor derives primitive thinking from that of children. Tylor takes for granted the famous Law of Recapitulation: that ontogeny recapitulates phylogeny. Children and therefore primitive adults animate all things: 'He who recollects when there was still personality to him in posts and sticks, chairs, and toys [and also one's own body parts], may well understand how the infant philosophy of mankind could extend the notion of vitality to what modern science only recognises as lifeless things.' Id., 2:62. Daube laments what he calls the nineteenth-century 'belief . . . in a progress of mankind from childishness to intelligence'. Daube (note 1), 245. But at least for Tylor, primitive peoples are intelligent, and they are so because for Tylor children are intelligent. Tylor respects primitive peoples and for that reason parallels their religion to our science.

culpability lie with a god who used any of these three as means. If Daube were to take the primitive stage of animism for Tylor as the measure of primitive, then he could easily argue that the biblical view — (a) by denying the animation of the hand, the axe, or the axe head; (b) by allowing for God to use one of these three as an inanimate means to God's end; or (c) by allowing for the accidental killing by a human — is far from primitive.

Tylor's characterization of primitive is scarcely the only one. Take anthropologist E. E. Evans-Pritchard's characterization in his *Witchcraft, Oracles and Magic among the Azande*.[28] For the Azande, according to Evans-Pritchard, science explains most physical events; religion — specifically, witchcraft — explains only unfortunate events, which means events that cause harm to others. To the Azande, the sheer physical features of a tree explain its ordinary, natural 'behaviour'. Witchcraft explains only unfortunate events involving the tree: why one day it falls on someone. In Evans-Pritchard's most famous example, witchcraft explains why a granary under which Azande are sitting collapses when it does. With unfortunate events, no room remains for chance, and even then the 'supernatural' explanation supplements, not supplants, the scientific-like explanation. For Evans-Pritchard, in contrast to Tylor, religion and science co-exist as explanations of events in the physical events, and they co-exist for both primitives and moderns. Thus the Azande readily attribute the collapse of an old granary to the gradual weakening of the wooden supports by termites, and likewise they attribute the presence of those sitting under the granary to a desire for shade during the heat of the day. But they invoke witchcraft to explain why this granary collapsed with this group of persons beneath it. Witchcraft connects what scientifically are independent, coincidental actions: the collapse of the granary with the presence of those sitting under it.[29]

---

[28] E. E. Evans-Pritchard, *Witchcraft, Oracles and Magic among the Azande* (Oxford 1937).
[29] See id., 69–70.

If Daube were to use Evans-Pritchard's conception of primitive, then there would be no accidental cases of harm, but there would be indirect ones. A stone over which one trips — and Evans-Pritchard himself cites an example of this kind — would not have positioned itself where it lay, as in primitive animism for Tylor. Rather, a witch would have done so. Hence indirect causation. (At the same time the witch would have been the actual antagonist of the victim and not, like Joab, an intermediary carrying out the will of the real antagonist.) But the harm would certainly have been intentional. Evans-Pritchard associates harm with atypicality — for example, with why, having walked along the same path many a time before, the boy trips over the stone just this time and, more, suffers a more severe injury than he would ordinarily have suffered for hitting his foot. Indeed, the Azande are prepared to forgo attributing at least the deaths of the elderly to witchcraft because all persons do die — even if most persons sitting under the granary do not.[30]

Daube mentions witchcraft in passing: 'At one time I wondered whether the laws against witches and the like were partly intended to render punishable misdeeds which would escape the very narrow definitions of other serious crimes. They would make it possible to get at the indirect author of death or injury.'[31] Daube is presumably asking whether laws against witchcraft were created to cover cases of culpability that fell outside laws that were restricted to direct causation. He does not name any of the laws, though witchcraft is certainly found in the Bible — most dramatically in the case of the witch of Endor (see 1 Samuel 28). In any event Azande witchcraft, if taken as illustrative of primitive thinking, precludes Daube's invocation of indirect causation as automatically 'post-primitive'. Evans-Pritchard's allowance for indirect but not accidental causation of harm makes Daube's linkage of direct with intentional simplistic.[32]

---

[30] See id., 26, 77.
[31] Daube (note 1), 251.
[32] Evans-Pritchard's discussion of witchcraft is so apt here because the Azande have a formal process for identifying the witch and securing compensation and ultimately overcoming social friction. That is, witchcraft is dealt with legally.

Tylor's characterization of 'primitive' reinforces Daube's argument that the biblical outlook is not primitive. Evans-Pritchard's challenges it. There are more radical characterizations than those of either Tylor or Evans-Pritchard — notably, that of the French philosopher Lucien Lévy-Bruhl, for whom primitives have no conception of causation itself. In any event Daube's paper would have been strengthened by an analysis of what might be meant by 'primitive'.

In another article, 'Error and Accident in the Bible',[33] Daube observes that outside of legal codes, the focus in the Bible and in ancient sources generally is on cases of error and not on cases of accident: 'So soon as we go outside the legal codes in the narrowest sense, into myth, saga, drama, historiography, we find interest exclusively concentrated on acts performed in error. Acts performed by accident play no part in reflections on human fate and responsibility.'[34] I do agree that in myth, where it is usually gods and not humans who are the agents, the emphasis is on intentional actions and so not on accidents. The emphasis on intent is exactly what for Tylor and others pits the personalistic explanation of myth against the impersonal (though not thereby accidental) explanation of science. What happens is what gods want to happen. Whenever there is regret, it is over error and not over accident. To cite the grandest example in the Bible, God sends the flood because he 'was sorry that he had made humankind on the earth' (Genesis 6:5). Certainly God, who is anything but omniscient, fails to anticipate many events — for example, Adam and Eve's eating from the Tree of Knowledge (see Genesis 3:22–23). Because error presupposes intent, the concentration on intent argues for, by this criterion, a primitive understanding of the world outside the law.

---

[33] D. Daube, 'Error and Accident in the Bible', *Revue Internationale des Droits de l'Antiquité*, 2 (1949), 189–213, republished in C. Carmichael, ed., *Biblical Law and Literature* [*Collected Works of David Daube*, 3] (Berkeley 2003), 359–74.
[34] Id., 190.

IV

Jacob's 'Red, Red Dish' and the Riddle of the Red Heifer

Calum Carmichael*

Historical events inspire biblical rituals, for example, the ritual of the Red Heifer. Esau sold his birthright for a 'red, red' dish that his brother Jacob cooked and that Esau wanted in order to fend off death because he thought it contained blood. Contact with blood contaminates, however, unless associated with the sanctuary. By burning an animal and its blood under the supervision of a priest and producing a purifying mixture of ashes mixed with water, the ritual imitates in order to oppose but similarly serves to counter fear about death. There are at least ten correspondences between the narrative in Genesis and the institution described in Numbers.

David Daube began his first book, *Studies in Biblical Law*,[1] by quoting a line from John Bunyan's *Pilgrim's Progress*, 'Would'st thou read Riddles, and their Explanation?' In what follows I attempt an explanation for a riddle that has baffled interpreters down the ages. Crucial to the solution, I will argue, is Daube's explanation of one of the puzzles he addressed in his book: how Jacob acquired the birthright from Esau. The incident is recounted in Genesis 25:20–34:

And Isaac was forty years old when he took Rebekah to wife, the daughter of Bethuel the Syrian of Padan-aram, the sister to Laban the Syrian. And Isaac intreated Yahweh for his wife, because she was barren: and Yahweh was

---

* Professor of Comparative Literature and Adjunct Professor of Law, Cornell University.
[1] Cambridge 1947.

Calum Carmichael, 'Jacob's "Red, Red Dish" and the Riddle of the Red Heifer', in E. Metzger, ed., *David Daube: A Centenary Celebration* (Glasgow: Traditio Iuris Romani, 2010), 48–70. Copyright © 2010 by Calum Carmichael (content) and Ernest Metzger (typographical arrangement). All rights reserved. ROMANLEGALTRADITION.ORG

intreated of him, and Rebekah his wife conceived. And the children struggled together within her; and she said, If it be so, why am I thus? And she went to inquire of Yahweh. And Yahweh said unto her, Two nations are in thy womb, and two manner of people shall be separated from thy bowels; and the one people shall be stronger than the other people; and the elder shall serve the younger. And when her days to be delivered were fulfilled, behold, there were twins in her womb. And the first came out red, all over like an hairy garment; and they called his name Esau. And after that came his brother out, and his hand took hold on Esau's heel; and his name was called Jacob: and Isaac was threescore years old when she bare them. And the boys grew: and Esau was a cunning hunter, a man of the field; and Jacob was a plain man, dwelling in tents. And Isaac loved Esau, because venison was in his mouth: but Rebekah loved Jacob. And Jacob cooked a stew: and Esau came from the field, and he was faint: And Esau said to Jacob, Feed me, I pray thee, with that red, red stuff; for I am faint: therefore was his name called Edom. And Jacob said, Sell me this day thy birthright. And Esau said, Behold, I am at the point to die: and what profit shall this birthright do to me? And Jacob said, Swear to me this day; and he sware unto him: and he sold his birthright unto Jacob. Then Jacob gave Esau bread and pottage of lentiles; and he did eat and drink, and rose up, and went his way: thus Esau despised his birthright.

The institution of the Red Heifer or Red Cow in Numbers 19 for dealing with those who have been in contact with corpses and the like is proverbial for its obscurity. Typical is *Numbers Rabba* on 19:3 (a medieval compilation) that has King Solomon say that while he understands the Torah's commandments, the one about the Red Heifer is quite beyond his comprehension. R. Johanan ben Zaccai (middle of the 1st century AD) expresses an earlier view when to outsiders he admits that magic seems to be involved. But he tells his disciples in private that neither is uncleanness caused by a corpse nor cleanness by the ritual's 'water of separation'. The statute was one of those that had to be accepted as the will of God even though no rational basis could be discerned even by the rabbis (*Pesiqta de Rab Kahana* 4:7).

The ritual is laid out in Numbers 19:1–22 and reads as follows in the translation of the King James Authorized Version (substituting 'Yahweh' for 'the Lord'):

And Yahweh spake unto Moses and unto Aaron, saying, This is the ordinance of the law which Yahweh hath commanded, saying, Speak unto the children of Israel, that they bring thee a red heifer without spot, wherein is no blemish, and upon which never came yoke: And ye shall give her unto Eleazar the priest, that he may bring her forth without the camp, and one shall slay her before his face: And Eleazar the priest shall take of her blood with his finger, and sprinkle of her blood directly before the tabernacle of the congregation seven times: And one shall burn the heifer in his sight; her skin, and her flesh, and her blood, with her dung, shall he burn: And the priest shall take cedar wood, and hyssop, and scarlet, and cast it into the midst of the burning of the heifer. Then the priest shall wash his clothes, and he shall bathe his flesh in water, and afterward he shall come into the camp, and the priest shall be unclean until the even. And he that burneth her shall wash his clothes in water, and bathe his flesh in water, and shall be unclean until the even. And a man that is clean shall gather up the ashes of the heifer, and lay them up without the camp in a clean place, and it shall be kept for the congregation of the children of Israel for a water of separation: it is a purification for sin. And he that gathereth the ashes of the heifer shall wash his clothes, and be unclean until the even: and it shall be unto the children of Israel, and unto the stranger that sojourneth among them, for a statute for ever. He that toucheth the dead body of any man shall be unclean seven days. He shall purify himself with it on the third day, and on the seventh day he shall be clean: but if he purify not himself the third day, then the seventh day he shall not be clean. Whosoever toucheth the dead body of any man that is dead, and purifieth not himself, defileth the tabernacle of Yahweh; and that soul shall be cut off from Israel: because the water of separation was not sprinkled upon him, he shall be unclean; his uncleanness is yet upon him. This is the law, when a man dieth in a tent: all that come into the tent, and all that is in the tent, shall be unclean seven days. And every open vessel, which hath no covering bound upon it, is unclean. And whosoever toucheth one that is slain with a sword in the open fields, or a dead body, or a bone of a man, or a grave, shall be unclean seven days. And for an unclean person they shall take of the ashes of the burnt heifer of purification for sin, and running water shall be put thereto in a vessel: And a clean person shall take hyssop, and dip it in the water, and sprinkle it upon the tent, and upon all the vessels, and upon the persons that were there, and upon him that touched a bone, or one slain, or one dead, or a grave: And the clean person shall sprinkle upon the unclean on the third day, and on the seventh day: and on the seventh day he shall purify himself, and wash his clothes, and bathe himself in water, and shall be clean at even. But the man that shall be unclean, and shall not purify himself, that soul shall be cut off from among the congregation, because he hath defiled the sanctuary of Yahweh: the water of separation hath not been sprinkled upon him; he is unclean. And it shall be a perpetual statute unto them, that he that sprinkleth the water of separation shall wash his clothes; and he that toucheth the water of separation shall be unclean until even. And whatsoever the unclean person toucheth shall be unclean; and the soul that toucheth it shall be unclean until even.

In order to consider the ritual in Numbers 19, I shall briefly review matters in Numbers 16–18. The major concern in that part of Numbers is the question of who controls the official cult. The outcome is that among the twelve tribes an elevated status is conferred on the tribe of Levi. Then a further distinction in rank is introduced. The larger body of Levites has a lesser standing than those Levites who are directly descended from Aaron's family. Thus in the prime position there are the priests, the Aaronites, responsible for the most sacred rites connected with the sanctuary — they enter the Tent of Meeting and officiate at it — and in a subsidiary role there are the Levites who are guardians of the sacred precinct. In larger perspective, after the events recorded in Genesis and part of Exodus, leadership in the sacred sphere comes about no longer mainly by direct divine intervention but indirectly through the persons of Aaron's family and the Levites. They embody the other brother tribes as Yahweh's firstborn.

Another issue that arises is: what dues should the Levites and the Aaronites receive? They turn out to be quite splendid, in keeping with the best part of an inheritance for the primary son: 'I [Yahweh] am thy part and thine inheritance among the sons of Israel' (Numbers 18:20). Their food comes from offerings to the sanctuary from the other Israelites. As a collective, the status of the priests and the Levites is, as just noted, that of Yahweh's firstborn son and even within this privileged position a distinction, as also just noted, is made between Aaron's family, the priests, and the other Levites. The distinction shows up in a particular distribution of food that comes initially from the tithes of the people. A tenth of this portion, the best part of it, must be given over by the Levites to the favoured priests. In a climactic statement there is a warning to the Levites about avoiding any profanation of this food 'lest you die' (Numbers 18:32). The final focus, then, is on one group of Levites serving their brother Levites, the sons of Aaron, by providing the latter with an especially sacrosanct tithe from threshing floor and winepress (vs. 27).

The Aaronites' attainment of paramount status came about in a struggle for power between, however ambiguously, one firstborn, the Levites, and another firstborn, the Aaronites, who proved to be superior. Numbers 16 and 17 depict this struggle which mirrors the similarly tension-laden interchange at the nation's origin when Esau, Isaac's firstborn, gives over the status of the firstborn to his brother, Jacob, who proves superior on the occasion. Esau's wrath at losing his birthright to his clever brother required God to protect Jacob who, in turn, pledged a tithe of all that the deity would give him in the future (Genesis 28:22). That tithe is the one under consideration in Numbers 18. Its mention is one indication that the Numbers narrator is alert at this point to

Jacob's history. This same history is the key to understanding the ritual of the Red Heifer because it dramatizes Esau's loss to Jacob.

Both the Levites and the Aaronites are held responsible for offences against the sacred: 'Thou [Aaron] and thy sons and thy father's house with thee shall bear the iniquity of the sanctuary: and thou and thy sons with thee shall bear the iniquity of your priesthood' (Numbers 18:1). As it happens, a sacred offence lies at the heart of how Israel became a nation on the occasion when Jacob acquired the birthright from Esau. That the Numbers narrator should turn to this momentous event is not in the least surprising. A primary feature of biblical lawmaking is that the laws take up issues arising in the nation's history, especially at its beginnings, with the laws incorporated into a coherent narrative that begins in Genesis and concludes in 2 Kings: from the creation of the world through the creation of the nation Israel to its end in exile in Babylon. Jacob, not Esau, became the firstborn in the line of Abraham and Isaac when Esau sought to eat a 'red, red' dish that Jacob was cooking and that Esau took to be a blood dish. He received instead a dish of red lentils. Esau's error, which involved a ruse by Jacob, prevented him from eating blood, which would have been an offence against the sacred order. But it also led to his losing the birthright to Jacob, who then became the father of the nation Israel.

Aside from a constant interest in exploring aspects of Israel as God's firstborn, why should the Numbers narrator turn to this particular episode? The reason is that the lawgiver needs to respond to the sacred offence at the heart of the story and does so by transforming it into a ritual for use not just by Jacob-Israel's descendants but Esau's too. Esau was famished and desperately needed to consume the blood dish in order to stave off the threat of death. Numbers 19 lays out a ritual that, imitating the situation in the story, opposes consumption of blood to fend off death and substitutes a ritually acceptable process involving blood to serve the same purpose. Because the ritual has been shrouded in mystery, I will examine in detail the way in which the Jacob-Esau narrative inspired its construction.

Genesis 25	Numbers 19
Encountering death. Jacob exploits Esau's craving for a blood dish to fend off death by giving him a red dish that, although lacking blood, keeps Esau alive.	*Encountering death.* A ritual that produces ashes from a red heifer, which has been burned with its blood and added red items, serves to ward off contamination by death.

Numbers 18 has to do with sanctuary matters in a major way but Numbers 19 only introduces the sanctuary in a curiously peripheral way. The concern is with a ceremony that commemorates the moment in Genesis 25, occurring long before the cult was officially established at Sinai, when Israel commenced on the path of firstbornhood with its culmination in the special role of Aaron's sons and the Levites. Although the ceremony is largely independent of the sanctuary — but not the priests — it does enact a sacred ritual involving blood.

Jacob's 'red, red' dish and the ritual of the Red Heifer. The ritual's puzzling features are manifest. Baruch Levine states: 'Numbers 19 provides a unique instance in priestly legislation of riddance rites separate from the Sanctuary and its sacrificial altar.' George Buchanan Gray states that 'the fact that the sacred victim is slaughtered outside the camp is quite exceptional, and is inconsistent with the view that it is a sacrifice, an offering to Yahweh.' Gray, like all other critics, also views the institution's placement in the Book of Numbers as decidedly problematical for no link is seen with what comes before or what comes after.[2] In the sequence, Numbers 18

---

[2] B. A. Levine, *Numbers 1-20* [Anchor Bible, 4A] (New York 1993), 470; G. B. Gray, *A Critical and Exegetical Commentary on the Book of Numbers* [The International Critical Commentary on the Holy Scriptures of the Old and New Testaments] (Edinburgh 1903), 250. On the problem of placement, Gray states: 'The present chapter, like c. 15, though it clearly belongs to P, has no intimate connection either with what precedes (c. 16-18 — the revolt of Korah) or with what follows (— the arrival at Kadesh).' Id., 241.

and 19, we move from the threat of death for wrongful eating of tabooed food, the tithe for the priests, to the law about applying the ashes of a red heifer to a person, Israelite or non-Israelite, who encounters death in the form of a corpse. How do we account for what seems a bewildering move? We have, indeed, to go back to an occasion at the very beginnings of the nation's history when Esau sought meat with blood that he usually obtained from his hunting expeditions. But such a dish is taboo because it is an offence against the sacred order. Eating meat with blood is contrary to the rule laid down for all humankind after the flood: one can eat meat but only after removing its blood and returning the blood to the deity (Genesis 9:3, 4). The move is from unlawful eating in Numbers 18 to a rule in Numbers 19 that is based on the narrative about Esau's potential act of wrongful eating.

Critics who say that there is no proper context for the institution of the ritual in Numbers have not been alive to the relevance of the Esau saga in Genesis 25. Not only is the issue of the firstborn a dominant theme in Numbers, but the quite particular topic of food and assistance to a firstborn via the agency of food is the concern in the texts that immediately precede the ritual of the Red Heifer. I consequently cannot agree with the critics. There is an especially close connection between Numbers 18 about sacred food for firstborn and Numbers 19 about the Red Heifer. Being alert to previous developments in the nation, the lawgiver, in Numbers 19, turns back to the food that Jacob gave Esau in place of a meat dish. At the time in question Esau was Isaac's firstborn but he was denied, after an unsuccessful hunt, his usual source of sustenance. The Red Heifer ritual enacts a recapitulation of and comment upon events in the story. Jacob's relationship to Esau is raised in the episode that occurs almost immediately after the institution of the Red Heifer. In Numbers 20, Moses has messengers request the King of Edom to permit Israel to pass through Edomite territory and the appeal is based on their original fraternal tie: 'Thus says your brother Israel' (Numbers 20:14). The reference is to the brothers

Jacob and Esau, precisely the two at the heart of the Red Heifer ritual.[3]

When we turn to the Numbers ritual, a major puzzle is: why must the animal be red in colour? Why is a colour mentioned at all? In attempting to make sense of the matter let me recall Gray's statement — although not made in regard to the Red Heifer ritual — that it is entirely in the manner of Priestly procedure 'to connect the origin of an institution with an event'.[4] This is true, I submit, for the institution of the Red Heifer. Esau, red in colour at birth and hairy to depict his later wild nature, becomes 'a man of the field', a hunter, while Jacob, gripping his brother's heel at birth to indicate that he will later supplant Esau's role in the family, becomes 'a tent-dweller'. One day Esau comes back from an unsuccessful hunting trip and is in a fearful state. As David Daube well demonstrates, Esau is depicted as desperately dependent on his game dishes with blood the central ingredient in them.[5] To Esau, blood has special, life-giving properties capable of reviving an exhausted hunter. The problem he confronts, I must emphasise, is not lack of food. He could easily obtain something to eat, let us say, roots or berries picked along the way. What he craves is the life force that supposedly comes from blood dishes.

Coincidentally with Esau's return from his hunt, or much more likely, opportunistically, Jacob is cooking a dish, the contents of which are not specified but are red in colour. Esau begs 'to gulp' some of, literally in Hebrew 'that red, red', that is, the redness of the dish is what is so important to him. Daube is correct to retain the double reference to the word 'red' in the Hebrew text.[6] When Esau asks permission not to eat but to gulp (*la'aṭ*) Jacob's food, the allusion may be to a

---

[3] There is a similar backward reference in Amos 1:11; cf. Deut 2:4. See N. H. Snaith, *Leviticus and Numbers* [*The Century Bible*] (London 1967), 277; E. W. Davies, *Numbers* [*New Century Bible Commentary*] (London and Grand Rapids, MI, 1995), 209.
[4] Gray (note 2), 384.
[5] Daube provides a detailed analysis of the episode in 'Summum Ius — Summa Iniuria', in *Studies in Biblical Law* (Cambridge 1947), 191–200, reprinted in C. Carmichael, ed., *Biblical Law and Literature* [*Collected Works of David Daube*, 3] (Berkeley 2003), 241–49.
[6] Daube (note 5), 195 (= *Biblical Law and Literature*, 244).

mode of eating comparable to a wild beast with its prey when it consumes the flesh with the blood. In post-biblical Hebrew, as Robert Alter points out, the verb *la'aṭ* is reserved for the feeding of animals. Further noting that the Hebrew text says that 'Isaac loved Esau for the game in his mouth' (Genesis 25:28), Alter wonders if the idiom alludes to 'Esau as a kind of lion bringing home game in its mouth'.[7] Esau is further described in Genesis 25:27 as 'a knowing hunter', and in Job 28:7 the same verb is used of a bird of prey.

In any event, Esau thinks that a meat dish is cooking on the fire, presumably from one of Jacob's domestic animals. The dish's red colour signifies to Esau the blood that is supposedly present in the pot and which he perceives as the substance he desperately needs to recover from his dire condition.[8] I repeat: it is the red in the dish on the stove that will save him from death, not just the food. Esau is quite specific when he asks to eat the red stew (with its blood) in order to live. It is at this point that Jacob suggests to Esau that he sell him his birthright.

The birthright is sold to Jacob. Esau believes that it is of no use to him because he is on the point of dying. Jacob has him swear to the transaction. Esau then finds that instead of receiving the revivifying blood dish he receives a paltry plate of red lentils. It is on account of the role the colour red plays in the transaction that Esau's name is changed to Edom (*'edom*), the 'red one'. In this context, the name evokes the Hebrew word for blood, *dam*. The same play upon words, *dam* and *'edom*, involving similar errors to Esau's, occurs in other contexts involving directly or indirectly his descendants, the Edomites: water made red by the sun shining on it is mistaken for blood and blood on God's garments is initially mistaken for red grape juice (2 Kings 3:20–22; Isaiah 34:5–7, 63:1–6).[9]

[7] R. Alter, *Genesis* (New York 1996), 128–29.
[8] Similar meals were the fare of the Spartan warriors and blood drawn from their horses the means of survival of the armies of Genghis Khan. In the *Odyssey*, the winner of the contest between the two beggars is to receive goat sausages and the disguised Odysseus eventually tastes one, which is 'bubbling with fat and blood' (Hom. *Od.* 18.55, 140).
[9] See K. A. Matthews, *Genesis 11:27–50:26* [*New American Commentary*, 1B] (Nashville, TN, 1996), 389.

Esau's change of name underlines just how much significance attaches to the redness of Jacob's dish and the confusion about its contents. Esau had become the firstborn son in a state of red. He loses the status by ingesting food of the same colour. A play upon words in Numbers 19:2 is not only similar to what appears in the story but also links the law to the story. The heifer has to be *'adumah temimah*: completely red.[10] In the Genesis story, Esau is ruddy (*'admoni*) all over and Jacob is *tam* (Genesis 25:25, 27), the same two words that describe the heifer. Also noteworthy is that Esau is 'red all over [*kulo*] like an hairy mantle' — conjuring up the image of a fully red creature. The description of the animal in the law points to the significant features of each brother (even if it is not clear what quality *tam* brings out in reference to Jacob). Esau's error about the animal meat comes to define his person: Edom is 'the red one', and Jacob is the civilized, *tam* man, the complete one or the one wholly man (in contrast to his animal-like brother), who knows how to exploit Esau's bestial need for blood.

We learn from Genesis 27:36 that Esau has no doubt that Jacob cheated him out of his birthright. A 'tripping up' describes both the purchase of the birthright in Genesis 25 and the theft of the blessing in Genesis 27 when he later took advantage of his father's blindness. In Genesis 25, Jacob exploits Esau's misperception about the contents of the 'red, red' dish by having him swear to a transaction that has Jacob give to Esau the dish in return for the status of the firstborn in the family. The sleight of hand consists, more precisely, in Jacob responding as if Esau had asked for any kind of red food, then exploiting the letter of their agreement and cyni-

---

[10] I take the two words together and do not put *temimah* with the following ones because doing so creates a redundant statement, 'without blemish [complete], in which there is no defect'. The Rabbis took the two words together but modern critics have typically put the second one, *temimah* (complete), with the next part of the sentence. They recognise the redundancy that arises but they claim it must be for emphasis. The Hebrew is literally, 'A cow red *temimah* in which there is no blemish in her'. See, for example, J. Milgrom, *Numbers* [*The Jewish Publication Society Torah Commentary*] (Philadelphia, PA, 1990), 158. His claim that Lev 22:21 has the 'identical construction' is simply not true. A possible link between the description of the heifer and the characteristics of Esau and Jacob has not been pointed out before.

cally making use of the realm of the numinous and the sacred. The swearing renders the deal beyond recall for by it the agreement enters the sphere of the absolute. Esau has no option but to accept the transaction of a birthright for a red dish that turns out to be lentils.[11]

For Jacob to make Esau swear an oath is not a strange step in the ordinary way of doing business. Behind an oath's sacrosanct nature is the serious matter that in a society lacking legal instruments a person's word is of enormous significance. What might appear odd from our perspective is quite rational within such a society. Jacob cleverly uses the oath because, noting that Esau has been careless in not checking exactly the food he desires, Jacob ensures that the transaction cannot be undone even though it involves underhandedness.

Esau's sale of his birthright to Jacob is a foundational moment in the history of the nation. All later developments about Israel's rescue from Egypt as God's firstborn son, and Israel's religious and sacrificial life as centered on the Levites representing that firstborn son (Numbers 3:40–51), begin with the episode in Genesis 25. From the point of view of the Book of Numbers, so concerned with primogeniture (Numbers 3:11–13, 40–51, 7, 8, 16–18, 26), the transaction between Esau and Jacob at the creation of the nation is of enormous interest and lies at the heart of the mysterious Red Heifer ritual in Numbers 19.

Response in Numbers 19 to the situation in Genesis 25. At the stage before its true contents (the lentils) emerge, Jacob's dish that Esau wanted would have been anathema from a priestly point of view to the lawgiver in Numbers because of its supposed blood content. Outside of the priests' use of blood in the sanctuary, blood dangerously contaminates. Only in associa-

---

[11] See Daube (note 5), 193–97 (= *Biblical Law and Literature,* 244–47). V. P. Hamilton, *The Book of Genesis 18–50* [*The New International Commentary on the Old Testament*] (Grand Rapids, MI, 1995), 186, cites Daube's solution to Jacob's cheating Esau but is mistaken in thinking that Daube weakens his argument by postulating an etymological link between *'adom* (red) and *dam* (blood). He does not. The link can be by sound alone. By drawing on Akkadian sources, Levine does argue for a link in meaning between the two words: Levine (note 2), 460.

tion with the sanctuary does blood have the opposite effect, absorbing and removing impurity.

In reacting negatively to the Genesis saga, the ritual-maker opposes the 'red, red' (blood) dish with a view to producing a mixture that, after any contact with death in the form of a corpse, or human bone or grave, will restore purity and hence life. The ritual imitates the fiction when Esau thinks that Jacob has slaughtered a domestic animal and cooked some of its meat without first removing the blood. Hebrew *parah*, heifer or probably more accurately, cow, is a term used loosely in biblical Hebrew for a domestic animal and certainly covers well the fictional beast Jacob had supposedly used to cook the 'red, red' dish over a fire.[12] Perhaps the animal's description in Numbers as *'adumah temimah* with its linguistic echo of a major characteristic of each brother is an appropriate way to draw attention to an animal that never existed. Esau thought that it did and Jacob pretended that it did, so it can be thought of as the non-existent *'adumah* (Esau) *temimah* (Jacob) animal. The ritual, we shall see, even enhances the red colour of the animal.

From Esau's perspective there is blood in Jacob's dish that comes from a slaughtered domestic animal. It is not true, but Jacob is content to have Esau think that it is. The red dish seems to contain blood and Jacob does not enlighten Esau as to its real nature. Indeed, Jacob seems fully prepared to be making a blood dish for eating and in the eyes of the Numbers lawgiver doing so would render him culpable along with Esau. As a result, the confusion (some think of it as deception) wins Jacob Esau's birthright. When we turn to the Red Heifer, as commentators well note, the designation of its colour is decidedly puzzling. It is a clue that something odd lies behind the ritual, in my view, Jacob's ruse with 'the red, red' dish.

The ritual incorporates a negative reaction to the supposed kind of meat dish Jacob cooks. The Numbers lawgiver's disapproval of Esau's and apparently Jacob's willingness to have him consume blood is one reason why the animal is burnt to ashes along with its blood. The requirement to burn

---

[12] See Levine (note 2), 461.

the blood of a slaughtered animal is unique to this law, 'something without parallel elsewhere in the Old Testament'.[13] The ritual highlights the redness, the quality falsely associated with blood in Jacob's preparation. The curious role of the colour red in the ritual picks up on the confusion caused by the dish's colour. In the first place, in the ritual, what exactly is a *red* heifer? Did such a fully red coloured animal actually exist? Most likely not (then as now),[14] and hence it is common to rationalize the problem away. Thus Jacob Milgrom has the colour as reddish-brown because, he states, brown cows are plentiful but a fully red one would not have existed or if it did, would have been extremely rare. But, then, why bother to designate a colour for the animal in the first place? Noth, while similarly rationalizing about the heifer's colour, is more alert to the problem when he writes about the animal: 'whose red (reddish-brown) color is obviously considered to be important for the intended effect' (to which he appends the statement: 'there is nothing in the Old Testament with which to compare this last point').[15]

The heifer's red colour really makes no sense because in the end the animal is totally incinerated and reduced to ashes. Yet, remarkably, the colour red is further highlighted by the explicit references to how its blood and its dung are burned and how a scarlet cloth is also thrown into the fire. Critics are probably correct in insisting that the Hebrew *piršah*, usually translated 'its dung', refers to its (bloody) entrails. Milgrom argues that cedar wood is used because its red colour symbolically adds to the quantity of blood in the ashes.[16] Yet the red ingredients eventually disappear into the

---

[13] G. J. Wenham, *Numbers* [*Tyndale Old Testament Commentaries*] (Leicester 1981), 146; Gray (note 2), 250; L. E. Binns, *The Book of Numbers* (London 1927), 127.
[14] L. Wright, Letter from Jerusalem, 'Forcing the End', *The New Yorker* (20 July 1998), 42, reports on an American cattle breeder who is attempting to produce a red heifer that is wholly red so that some contemporary Jews and Christians can produce the ashes from it in order to usher in the Messianic era (according to their understanding of the biblical ritual).
[15] M. Noth, *Numbers* [*Old Testament Library*] (Philadelphia, PA, 1968), 140; Milgrom (note 10), 158; also W. K. Gilders, 'Why Does Eleazar Sprinkle the Red Cow Blood? Making Sense of a Biblical Ritual', *Journal of Hebrew Scriptures*, 6 (2006), 2.
[16] Gray (note 2), 253; Binns (note 13), 127; Milgrom (note 10), 440 (see also 158).

fire, so we have to wonder all the more why redness comes into the ritual at all. The highlighting of the colour seems an unnecessary, gratuitous facet of the ritual. The resulting (cold) ashes will not be red, so the role of redness has no obvious relevance.

The colour is highlighted because it harks back to the role of the colour red in the episode in Genesis 25. In Jacob's cooking activity no animal is, in fact, involved but in an illusory way the redness of the dish indicates to Esau that one is. If Esau had not mistaken what the redness in Jacob's dish signified, the transaction of the sale of the birthright would not have taken place. In the final outcome of the Genesis story (as in the ritual), the colour has little or no relevance. Esau finds out that the redness comes from lentils and not from the blood of an animal for which he has a craving.

We can also explain another major puzzle: while the function of the burnt heifer is to purify those defiled by death in some form, the burning process defiles those doing so. The animal confers uncleanness on the lay person burning the animal, on the priest who casts into the fire the cedar wood, the hyssop, and the scarlet material, and on the lay person gathering its ashes. These participants in the ritual become unclean on account of their duties and remain so until, by undergoing cleansing with water, they achieve purification in the evening. Why do they become unclean? In effect, they mirror the original potential offence in Genesis because they do not remove the animal's blood in accordance with priestly law. That is, in mimicking the scene with Esau and Jacob, they become unclean by association with the failure on the part of Esau, certainly, and Jacob, possibly, to recognise that blood must always be totally drained from a dead animal and cannot be eaten with its flesh.

Why is the ritual 'a purification for sin' (Numbers 19:9)? Milgrom and Wright argue, despite many indications to the contrary, that we are in fact dealing with a sacrifice. The ashes act as a prospective purification or purgation offering for later use on account of human remains. Somehow the blood retains its power even though it has been burnt. One problem with this view, which I do not entirely discount, is that it is odd to think that blood subject to conflagration still retains its power. Another problem is that, as they well recognise, the animal is slaughtered outside the camp by a non-priest, its blood is not splashed over the altar, and the use of cedar, hyssop, and scarlet material, as here, is never found in sacrifices. The term used for its ashes is *ʾeper* (vs. 9) and *ʿapar* (vs. 17), not *dešen* as in the ashes left after a cultic offering. Noth says of the statement about the removal of sin by the cow's ashes that 'it is left hanging in the air and is all the more surprising since a sacrificial action has precisely not taken place.' Noth sees the statement as an addition but gives no reason why a scribe bothered to add it.[17] The slaughtered animal is simply not a sacrificial offering. Rather, in my view, the ritual is meant to recall a historical moment associated with the original ancestor Jacob and attacks the unacceptable willingness to consume a meat dish with blood in it as portrayed in the narrative.

In sum, for the Numbers lawgiver, representing a priestly perspective, the incident in which Jacob acquires the right of the firstborn presents an objectionable belief about blood. The redness of the heifer in the ritual is crucial because the law's focus is on the supposed magical effect of the 'red, red' dish. The magic here is Esau's wrongful idea that he can control his world by attributing a power to blood that it does not have outside of its use by a priest within the sanctuary. By reducing the animal to ashes under the supervision of a priest (Eleazar), the lawgiver has the redness attaching to the cow totally obliterated in order to oppose the power attributed to the blood that Esau thinks is in Jacob's dish.

Positive significance of the ritual. Just as the Day of Atonement by ritualized actions turns the evil of Joseph's brothers'

---

[17] Noth (note 15), 140; Milgrom (note 10), 438–41; D. P. Wright, ed., *Anchor Bible Dictionary*, 3 (New York 1992), 115. See the criticism of their position by Davies (note 3), 197, 199–200; Albert Baumgarten sees no link with the parallel rituals Milgrom cites in ancient Near Eastern sources, and finds 'patently implausible' the argument that the ashes constitute a ritual detergent that prospectively absorbs the impurities to which they will be applied: A. I. Baumgarten, 'The Paradox of the Red Heifer', *Vetus Testamentum*, 43 (1993), 444; also Gilders' criticism of Milgrom's understanding of Eleazar's action with the blood (Gilders (note 15), 9).

deed with a slaughtered goat into good,[18] so the creator of the ritual in Numbers, responding negatively to how Jacob attained the birthright from Esau, exploits the incident for a positive use. The beneficial aspect of the Red Heifer ritual he derives from the idea that is central to the story: Esau's need to keep death at bay. Because no animal is actually used in Genesis 25, Jacob's deception inspires the question: how might a slaughtered animal serve to repel death (other than by eating it without its blood)? The move is comparable to the one that lies behind the construction of the Day of Atonement in Leviticus 16 when a live goat that is sent to the demonic being Azazel ('Mighty Goat') in the wilderness represents the non-existent wild beast that killed Joseph. Similarly inventing the ritual in Numbers 19, the lawgiver takes the fictitious animal killed in Genesis 25, suggests an actual slaughtered animal, and emphasises the primary feature associated with Jacob's make-believe, that is, the red colour that caused Esau to put aside his fear of death.

The ritual applies to various instances in which an Israelite or a resident non-Israelite encounters death: touching a corpse, entering a tent or being near an open vessel in a tent that has been exposed to a corpse, touching someone in open fields who has been slain by a sword or who has died naturally, or touching a human bone, or a grave (Numbers 19:14–16). There is opposition to one use of animal blood, as food for Esau, with a view to exploiting its use in another acceptable way, as a counter to the miasma of death. The two cases of death cited in the ritual concern death in a tent and death in the open field. Noteworthy is the fact that in the story Jacob is a 'tent-dweller' and Esau is a 'man of the field': 'And Esau was a knowing hunter, a man of the field; and Jacob was a complete man, dwelling in tents' (Genesis 25:27). The prey-deprived, death-fearing Esau comes from the open field and receives from the tent-dweller Jacob the death-defying red dish.

A human corpse is manifestly like animal meat that has not had the blood thoroughly and immediately removed from

---

[18] See C. Carmichael, 'The Origin of the Scapegoat Ritual,' *Vetus Testamentum*, 50 (2000), 167–82.

it. Both human corpse and animal carcass contaminate; in Howard Eilberg-Schwartz's terms, each represents not just something dead but additionally 'death' itself that is impurity.[19] For the lawgiver, blood does indeed repel death but it can only do so if it is linked to the sanctuary. Blood under the control of the priests is associated with life and is thought to ward off death. Central to the positive role of the ritual is the action by the priest at the beginning when he takes some of the newly slain animal's blood on his finger and sprinkles it seven times in the direction of the sanctuary (Numbers 19:4). The action plainly signifies some removal, however little, of blood from a slaughtered animal. Its symbolic transfer from the animal in the direction of the sanctuary will be on the ground that 'the blood is the life' (Deuteronomy 12:23; Genesis 9:4) and should properly return to the deity who resides in the sanctuary.

The placement of some of the ashes from the burnt, previously blood sodden dead animal in the 'water of separation' (*me niddah*) serves an efficacious function. The mixture of ashes and water achieves its end in a manner not open to rational scrutiny, just as lentils boiled in water over a fire keeps death from Esau but in a manner that is also seemingly magical because of the redness attaching to the dish. The fact that the heifer before its slaughter is without blemish and never bore a yoke already indicates that the animal is to be put to a positive use (Numbers 19:2). David Wright thinks that because a firstling could not have a yoke put on it (Deuteronomy 15:19), the heifer may well have been a firstborn animal, a point of some interest given the issue of primogeniture that dominates both the story in Genesis 25 and the context in Numbers.[20]

On the one hand, then, there is recall of the fiction of Jacob killing an animal and opposition to what he supposedly made from it, namely, a blood dish capable of giving life to an expiring Esau. On the other hand, there is the affirmative action of reducing an animal to ashes and preserving them with a view to achieving the end that Esau sought and Jacob

---

[19] H. Eilberg-Schwartz, *The Savage in Judaism* (Bloomington, IN, 1984), 188.
[20] *Anchor Bible Dictionary* (note 17), 3:115.

supported, namely, resisting the realm of death. Certainly not resistance to impending death by eating blood but a different application: to counter the fear of a corpse and the like.

The law's reference to less unusual situations evoking death than Esau's plight is illuminating. Just as Esau's fear of dying from the failure to obtain his beloved meat-with-blood food is irrational (he could have eaten anything, not just meat, to ward off starvation), so too is the fear generated by a corpse, a tent or an open vessel infected by a corpse, a human bone, or a grave. In each instance, moreover, it is the red quality attaching to, respectively, Jacob's dish in the story and the heifer in the law that is the decisive element in addressing the problem. A notable gap between story and law prevails. Esau's sense of urgency stands in stark contrast with the long duration and delay built into the ritual. To counter the contamination of death a sprinkling of the water of separation on the affected person does not occur until the third day. Four days later there is a second and final sprinkling. A hurried response to the presence or reminder of death is absent. The feature of a third day sprinkling and another on the seventh day is unique.

The seemingly magical element is not, however, the important feature of the ritual. The crucial aspect is the dramatization of a foundational moment in the life of the nation. The law has no historical reality in the sense of reflecting the ongoing cultic life of the Israelite nation. Its incorporation of a past event is where a historical dimension lies. We are not dealing with a law as a legislative statute, but with a law that is more like a statue that emblematically recalls and commemorates the past.

Numbers 16 and 17 provide a good parallel to the emblematical nature of the law of the Red Heifer. First there is a narrative incident to be commemorated: Moses has rebels led by the Levite Korah fill censers with fire and incense to see whether their claim to have equal status with the Aaronite priests is justified. It proves a wrongful claim and they perish by fire. There follows the commemoration: the censers, flattened into a casing, are kept in the sanctuary in the form of the altar's copper covering to recall the offence in Moses' own time. The institution of the ritual of the Red Heifer serves the same commemorative function but because the incident occurs in Jacob's lifetime, and not during Moses', the original occasion is not explicitly cited. To contribute to the fiction that Moses delivers the laws, only events in his lifetime and not those that occur before or after it are ever cited in the laws (for instance, the obvious lack of reference to King Solomon in the prohibition that the king not multiply horses, wives, silver and gold in Deuteronomy 17:14–20 or the comparable lack of reference to Rachel and Leah in the rule about upholding the right of a hated wife's first-born son in Deuteronomy 21:15–17.).

The ritual of the Red Heifer is a product of reflection on Israelite tradition and I doubt has anything to do with a transformation of some remote, pre-Israelite rite of exorcism for dealing with contamination coming from corpses and the like. Such rites may well have existed in the lawgiver's time, but if they did they are probably not especially relevant to the ritual of the Red Heifer. My view stands in sharp contrast with other scholars'. Milgrom assumes some such biblical transformation and postulates that 'the demonic impurity of corpses of a bygone rite has been devitalized.' Noth also assumes that some primitive, magical rite has been transformed with the introduction of Israelite priestly supervision of it. The supposed primitive stage 'has been brought into at least an outward connection with the legitimate (Yahweh) cult.' S. Wefing argues that the ritual was originally a form of ordeal inveighing against pagan sacrifice. Roland de Vaux writes, 'This rite certainly originated in pagan practices, and it must have been originally a magic rite.' Paul Mpungu Muzinga provides a summary and negative critique of the view that we are dealing with some primitive rite that has been surprisingly preserved. The Numbers ritual is not, he concludes, 'une "survivance", lequel faisait partie des "pratiques archaïques et magiques" que les Hébreux ont hérité et ont assimilé à un "sacrifice d'expiation pour le péché".'[21]

---

[21] Milgrom (note 10), 443, taking up from Gray (note 2), 244–45; Noth (note 15), 141; S. Wefing, 'Beobachtungen zum Ritual der roten Kuh (Num. 19 1–10a)', *Zeitschrift für die Alttestamentliche Wissenschaft*, 93 (1981), 341–

The ritual of the Red Heifer is an invention inspired by the transaction between Jacob and Esau about the privilege of being firstborn. It is doubtful that the ritual was ever intended for institutional realization. For one thing, as Eryl Davies points out, in other texts washing in water alone was sufficient for a priest to remove contamination associated with an animal carcass (Leviticus 5:2, 5–13; 11:24–28) or a human corpse (Leviticus 22:4–6): 'It is not clear why this particular method of lustration should have been instigated at all, for provisions elsewhere in the OT indicate that washing in plain water was sufficient to remove any contamination incurred by contact with the dead.'[22] Roland de Vaux notes that biblical texts describing funerary rites 'do not remotely suggest that contact with a corpse brings on defilement (cf. especially Genesis 46:4, 50:1).' He puts forward the odd argument that the Red Heifer ritual is an archaic rite that was not part of the ordinary life of the people but somehow lived on side by side with the official religion.[23] In my view, the institution in Numbers 19 is a hypothetical construction that is specifically derived from the Genesis story and hence a product of an ancient scribal school's project of integrating narrative and law in Genesis – 2 Kings.

The ritual reenactment of what takes place between Jacob and Esau, that is, Israel and Edom, applies to non-Israelites too (Numbers 19:10), and Levine is much struck by the inclusion of a resident alien in the rule.[24] But Edomites, the descendants of Esau, who might choose to reside in Israel, would fall into this category and therefore it is less of a surprise that the resident alien comes into consideration. In the ongoing narration of events in Numbers, the Edomites' encounter with the Israelites in the wilderness next comes into reckoning (Numbers 20:14–29).

The one other biblical source outside of Numbers in which there is mention of the ritual is Ezekiel 36:25 and, signifi-

---

64; R. de Vaux, *Ancient Israel*, 2 (New York 1965), 461; and P. Mpungu Muzinga, *La pratique des Rituels de Nombres 19 pendant la période hellénistique et romaine* (Pendé 2008), 45.

[22] Davies (note 3), 193.
[23] de Vaux (note 21), 2:462.
[24] Levine (note 2), 464–65.

cantly, Edom again plays a prominent role. There is reference, in particular, to the ancient enmity between Edom and Israel, that is, to the struggle between Esau and Jacob (Ezekiel 35:5–6). There are references also to the judgment upon the nations, with Edom the only nation singled out by name (Ezekiel 36:5), and to the blood that defiled the land of Israel (Ezekiel 36:16–21). Ezekiel, who is well familiar with priestly lore, speaks metaphorically of how the Red Heifer ritual will cleanse Israel after it has experienced its enemies' destructive power, that is, when Edom took possession of its land, which the Israelites themselves had previously defiled with blood. Like the original Jacob and Esau in dealing with 'the red, red' dish, there is joint guilt.

Some more general points may be set down by way of overall summary. How Jacob achieved top status in his family surely demanded attention among those who surveyed Israelite beginnings. It is, therefore, not surprising that the incident comes to expression in seemingly mysterious elements of a ritual. It is generally true, especially in law, that the more important the subject matter, the transfer of primogeniture, for instance, the more it is likely to attract ritualistic forms. The transfer of land is another example that attracts them (cf. Ruth 4:7).

As is common the world over, rituals often embody the reversal of an unwelcome situation and the ritual of the Red Heifer, which imitates in order to recall and oppose, is but another example. Somewhat comparable is how the bow that appears in the cloud after the Flood (Genesis 9:13) originally represents the bow with which God wages his battles (Exodus 15:3; Habakkuk 3:9, 11). Its placement in the cloud is a sign that God has ceased his hostilities against man.[25]

The magic associated with the Red Heifer ritual is really not magic at all but is about dramatizing Esau's desire for a

---

[25] On rituals with acts that are analogous to those they are designed to counter, see C. Lévi-Strauss, *The Raw and the Cooked* (New York 1969), 335–36; also D. P. Wright, *The Disposal of Impurity: Elimination Rites in the Bible and in Hittite and Mesopotamian Literature* [Society of Biblical Literature, Dissertation series, 101] (Atlanta, GA, 1987), 39–43. On the rainbow, see M. Weinfeld, *Deuteronomy and the Deuteronomic School* (Oxford 1972), 205, 206.

bloody meat dish with Jacob's collusion. After all, deceiving the senses is what magic is about and once we are undeceived the magic vanishes. To speak of a magical component as characterizing the ritual, as has been the universal judgment, is a confession of bewilderment about strange practices. The bafflement disappears when we view the ritual of the Red Heifer (like those of the Passover and the Day of Atonement) as a dramatic retelling of a foundational story, which by its very nature consists of a highly unusual happening.

There is, to be sure, a magical factor to be evaluated in Esau's situation. What saves him from dying is not just the partaking of food in the form of lentils, but his belief in the magical properties of the 'red, red' dish. There is a strange element in Esau's situation: yes, he needs food but he needs, from his viewpoint, much more than food. He gets the lentils but not the magical ingredient, blood. The situation is derisory and in this light he deserves to be despised for giving up his birthright (Genesis 25:34). The narrative, like the ritual, condemns Esau.

In sum, Genesis 25 and Numbers 19 share a considerable number of correspondences. There is the appeal to the fraternal relationship between Jacob and Esau in the episode that follows the establishment of the Red Heifer ritual. There is blood in the story that is suggested and emphasised by the red dish and there is blood in the ritual. Certain food, meat with blood, the slaughtered animal with its blood almost wholly intact, is taboo in each. Potential contamination caused by blood in the story has its opposite in the purifying mixture of ashes and water in the law. Fire is common to both texts. Redness is highlighted in both. The fear of death is central to both. Indeed, if we had to capture the curious outcome both of the Genesis narrative and the rule in Numbers 19, we might borrow the words of Virginia Woolf: 'I meant to write about death, only life came breaking in as usual.'[26] There is a sacred component in both: in the narrative, Esau's oath, and in the ritual, priestly supervision of the entire proceedings. The interest in the firstborn is part of

---

[26] A. O. Bell, ed., *The Diary of Virginia Woolf*, 2 (London 1978), 167 (17 February 1922).

each context: in Genesis, after a struggle that began in their mother's womb, Esau loses his firstborn status and in the Book of Numbers, after a struggle that is detailed before the laying out of the ritual, the Levites attain the status of God's firstborn. Jacob's status as firstborn is initially linked to vegetable food, lentils, which sustain Esau's life in the face of death. The institution of the ashes of the Red Heifer serves a similar function of affirming life in the midst of death. The institution, moreover, comes immediately after a rule regarding vegetable food, the special tithe, which gives life to another kind of firstborn, the higher priestly class. Finally, both story and ritual share an interest in a domestic animal, illusory in the story, seemingly real in the ritual but for the following reason I think illusory also.

The ritual is invented tradition to record the narrator's judgment on a crucial but decidedly questionable event at the nation's beginning. When commentators recognise that red heifers or cows never existed they do not conclude that the ritual probably did not exist either. Instead, they rationalize the problem away by suggesting other colours. Their unquestioned assumption is that the biblical texts must reflect real life in ancient Israel. I think that is an unsafe assumption. Numbers 19 is not a historical archive but a literary composition.

V

Law, Narrative and Theology: Daube on the Prodigal Son

Bernard Jackson[*]

This essay revisits David Daube's halakhic analysis of Luke's Parable of the Prodigal Son, noting that the original division did not apply to after-acquired property. Unusually, DD here confined himself to the halakhic questions; I add some comments, in the spirit of DD's approach elsewhere to the Jewish background to the New Testament, on the theological issues of atonement and forgiveness, and the referential message in relation to the membership and status of the new Church. At all three levels, the parable's conclusion is that there is a problem not yet fully resolved: the returning prodigal does not supplant his older brother; his precise ultimate inheritance remains to be decided. So too as regards his atonement and forgiveness: the returnee's motivation is not questioned: we shall see how he gets on. Similarly, with pagan converts to Christianity: circumcision is not immediately (if at all) required. The weak institutionalisation of inheritance law at this time is thus matched by flexibility in the theology and organisation of the early Church.

My studies with David Daube focused on the Hebrew Bible and its rabbinic interpretation,[1] with only incidental forays into the New Testament. In more recent years, however, I have come to a particular appreciation of the latter side of his

---

[*] Professor of Law and Jewish Studies, Liverpool Hope University.
[1] My doctoral thesis was published as *Theft in Early Jewish Law* (Oxford 1972).

Bernard Jackson, 'Law, Narrative and Theology: Daube on the Prodigal Son', in E. Metzger, ed., *David Daube: A Centenary Celebration* (Glasgow: Traditio Iuris Romani, 2010), 71–87. Copyright © 2010 by Bernard Jackson (content) and Ernest Metzger (typographical arrangement). All rights reserved. ROMANLEGALTRADITION.ORG

work. It is there, I would suggest, that we find the most profound synthesis of DD's interests — not only the sources he used (Hebrew Bible, intertestamental literature, New Testament, classics) — but also the approaches he brought to them: the technical legal (halakhic), the relationship of law and narrative (aggadic), and the theological. Here, however, I focus on a NT text where David confined himself to the halakhic issues, and will attempt to paint a broader picture, encompassing also the narrative and theological issues. In so doing, I draw also on insights offered by two other alumni, Reuven Yaron and Calum Carmichael.[2]

The passage I shall here briefly discuss[3] is the famous parable of the prodigal son, found (only) in Luke. As rendered in the RSV, we read:

Luke 15:

11 And he said, There was a man who had two sons;
12 and the younger of them said to his father, 'Father, give me the share of property that falls to me.' And he divided his living between them.
13 Not many days later, the younger son gathered all he had and took his journey into a far country, and there he squandered his property in loose living.
14 And when he had spent everything, a great famine arose in that country, and he began to be in want.
15 So he went and joined himself to one of the citizens of that country, who sent him into his fields to feed swine.
16 And he would gladly have fed on the pods that the swine ate; and no one gave him anything.
17 But when he came to himself he said, 'How many of my father's hired servants have bread enough and to spare, but I perish here with hunger!
18 I will arise and go to my father, and I will say to him, Father, I have sinned against heaven and before you;
19 I am no longer worthy to be called your son; treat me as one of your hired servants.'
20 And he arose and came to his father. But while he was yet at a distance, his father saw him and had compassion, and ran and embraced him and kissed him.
21 And the son said to him, 'Father, I have sinned against heaven and before you; I am no longer worthy to be called your son.'
22 But the father said to his servants, 'Bring quickly the best robe, and put it on him; and put a ring on his hand, and shoes on his feet;

---

[2] Nor should we overlook the contribution to this topic of the current holder of David's chair, A. J. B. Sirks, 'The Prodigal Son', *Journal of Legal History*, 25/2 (2005), 151–60, who views (at 151–53) the story against Roman legal and ethical concerns with the *luxuriosus*.

[3] My full account of this passage is published as 'The Jewish Background to the Prodigal Son: An Unresolved Problem', in B. S. Jackson, *Essays on Halakhah in the New Testament* (Leiden 2008), 111–50.

23 and bring the fatted calf and kill it, and let us eat and make merry;
24 for this my son was dead, and is alive again; he was lost, and is found.' And they began to make merry.
25 Now his elder son was in the field; and as he came and drew near to the house, he heard music and dancing.
26 And he called one of the servants and asked what this meant.
27 And he said to him, 'Your brother has come, and your father has killed the fatted calf, because he has received him safe and sound.'
28 But he was angry and refused to go in. His father came out and entreated him,
29 but he answered his father, 'Lo, these many years I have served you, and I never disobeyed your command; yet you never gave me a kid, that I might make merry with my friends.
30 But when this son of yours came, who has devoured your living with harlots, you killed for him the fatted calf!'
31 And he said to him, 'Son, you are always with me, and all that is mine is yours.
32 It was fitting to make merry and be glad, for this your brother was dead, and is alive; he was lost, and is found.'

In an article first published in 1955,[4] Daube sought to understand the property/inheritance relationships reflected in the parable. He saw very clearly that the initial division of the father's estate involved two distinct forms of transaction, reflecting the fact that the older son would remain at home, alongside the father, while the younger sought to leave the father's household, perhaps permanently. The younger son thus needed an arrangement in which he had immediate, unrestricted access to his entitlement, while the older son had no such need. Early rabbinic law, Daube noted, distinguished along these lines between different forms of gift. On the one hand, there was the *matanat bari* (suitable for the older son), in which the father retained a usufruct in the property, while giving future ownership (on his death) to the son;[5] on the

---

[4] D. Daube, 'Inheritance in Two Lukan Pericopes', *Zeitschrift der Savigny-Stiftung für Rechtsgeschichte* (rom. Abt.), 72 (1955), 326–34, reprinted in C. Carmichael, ed., *New Testament Judaism* [*Collected Works of David Daube*, 2] (Berkeley 2000), 807–15.

[5] M. *Baba Batra* 8:7(a):

> If a man assigned his goods to his sons he must write, 'From today and after my death'. So R. Judah. R. Jose says: He need not do so. If a man assigned his goods to his son to be his after his death, the father cannot sell them since they are assigned to his son, and the son cannot sell them since they are in the father's possession. If his father sold them, they are sold [only] until he dies; if the son sold them, the buyer has no claim on them until the father dies. The father may pluck up [the crop of a field which he has assigned] and

other hand, there was an outright gift, an 'advance', which, according to the Mishnah, was *not* taken into account in any final distribution of the estate;[6] so that the donee was not thereby disinherited, but rather remained a potential heir.

It was against this background that we should seek to understand the family tensions which developed on the prodigal's return. But the result of so doing does not appear to resolve all the problems. To be sure, the older son may have a complaint that the asset of the fatted calf was 'liquidated' without his being consulted, thereby prejudicing his future interest in it. But the father's response appears to go beyond this: 'all that is mine is yours' (vs. 31), suggesting that the issue involves the ultimate distribution of the father's estate. This raises two questions: (1) had not the full estate already been committed, so that the half which had not been squandered by the prodigal was already in the older son's hands?; (2) in seeking to reassure the older son, contrary to the implications of the mishnaic rule regarding the 'advance', was the father in fact alluding to an alternative halakhic tradition, according to which the giving of an advance (especially when the donee left the paternal household) did involve a disinheritance?

The answer to the first question involves a rule which Daube did not mention in his analysis. The *matanat bari* applied only to property then in the father's possession, and did not extend to after-acquired property.[7] Thus, while the older son was in principle secure in what his father had

> give to eat to whom he will, and if he left anything already plucked up, it belongs to [all] his heirs.

6   M. *Baba Batra* 8:7(b):

> If he left older sons and younger sons, the older sons may not care for themselves [out of the common inheritance] at the cost of the younger sons, nor may the younger sons claim maintenance at the cost of the older sons, but they all share alike. If the older sons married [and drew upon the common inheritance] the younger sons may marry [and draw in like manner]. If the younger sons said, 'We will marry [on the same scale] as ye married [when our father was yet alive]', they do not listen to them; for *what their father had given them, he has given.*

7   *Tosefta Ketubbot* 8:5: 'Whoever assigns his goods to his son and then acquires other goods — anything not included in the (first) gift belongs to the heirs.'

already given him,[8] he had legitimate concerns about the future distribution of the residual estate, now that the prodigal had (perhaps unexpectedly) reappeared on the scene. That makes the second question all the more pertinent: had the prodigal in fact returned as a potential heir, or not?

At this point, an important methodological issue arises. Do we seek to interpret the Lukan parable by means of rabbinic sources which are significantly later, or do we use the parable as evidence of an early halakhic tradition, not adopted by the Mishnah? Here, in fact, Daube was able to point to later reflections of that 'deviant' rule in rabbinic literature and concluded that the Lukan parable does reflect (in the father's response) awareness of that tradition. But he was also able to point to a clear instance of disinheritance by making an 'advance' in the Hebrew Bible itself. Genesis 25:5–6 gives the following account of the succession to Abraham:

> Abraham gave all he had to Isaac. But to the sons of his concubines[9] Abraham gave gifts, and while he was still living he sent them away from his son Isaac, eastward to the east country.

Clearly, these sons to whom Abraham gave advances were not expected to return and claim a share in the ultimate inheritance. The rabbinic commentary on this passage in *Genesis Rabbah* is cited by Daube[10] in support of the view that the initial grant to the prodigal did exclude the prodigal from any further interest in his father's estate:[11]

> In the days of Alexander of Macedon the Ishmaelites came to dispute the birthright with Israel . . . . Said Alexander of Macedon to them: 'Who is the

---

[8] The *matanat bari* conferred a 'vested' (irrevocable) interest, since the grant could not, in this period, be revoked: *Tosefta Baba Batra* 8:10; R. Yaron, *Gifts in Contemplation of Death in Jewish and Roman Law* (Oxford 1960), 51–55. Later, it could (as in a modern will). See further I. Grunfeld, *The Jewish Law of Inheritance* (Southfield, MI, 1987), 103.

[9] Mention having just been made of Keturah and her offspring: Gen 25:1–4. From the fact that the Hebrew is plural, and that Ishmael is mentioned shortly afterwards (Gen 25:9) as having joined Isaac in burying Abraham, rabbinic interpretation takes the *pilagshim* to refer to Keturah and Hagar and their sons as including Ishmael. See, inter alia, *Midrash Rabbah* (LXI:7) on Gen 25:6, quoted below.

[10] Daube, *New Testament Judaism* (note 4), 812f.

[11] *Midrash Rabbah* (LXI:7) on Gen 25:6. Translation of H. Freedman, *Midrash Rabbah*, 2 (London 1939), 545–46.

plaintiff, and who the defendant?' Said the Ishmaelites: 'We are the claimants, and we base our claim on their own laws. It is written, *But he shall acknowledge the firstborn, the son of the hated*, etc. (Deut. XXI, 17), and Ishmael was the firstborn.' Said Gebiah, the son of Kosem: 'Your Majesty! Cannot a man do as he wishes to his sons?' 'Yes', replied he. 'Then', pursued he, 'surely it is written, *And Abraham gave all that he had unto Isaac*' (Gen. XXV, 5).' 'But where is the deed of gift [to his other sons]?'[12] He replied: 'BUT UNTO THE SONS OF THE CONCUBINES, THAT ABRAHAM HAD, ABRAHAM GAVE GIFTS.' Thereupon they departed in shame.

An even stronger argument for the antiquity of disinheritance by making an advance may be derived from a different, and probably earlier, version of this same debate[13] before Alexander, found in the Babylonian Talmud, *Sanhedrin* 91a. This version is more explicit in taking the gifts to the children of Keturah as excluding them from any further inheritance:

On another occasion the Ishmaelites and the Ketureans came for a lawsuit against the Jews before Alexander of Macedon. They pleaded thus: 'Canaan belongs jointly to all of us, for it is written, Now these are the generations of Ishmael, Abraham's son; and it is [further] written, And these are the generations of Isaac, Abraham's son.' Thereupon Gebiha b. Pesisa ... pleaded against them. 'Whence do ye adduce your proof?' asked he. 'From the Torah', they replied. 'Then I too', said he, 'will bring you proof only from the Torah, for it is written, And Abraham gave all that he had unto Isaac. But unto the sons of the concubines which Abraham had, Abraham gave gifts: if a father made a bequest[14] to his children in his lifetime and sent them away from each other, has one any claim upon the other? [Obviously not.]'

Daube mentions further institutions whereby 'in certain periods and regions at least, contrary to orthodox Talmudic law, a Jewish father could transfer a portion of his goods to a son, thereby ending any further claims of the latter.'[15] Of particular interest (though our ultimate judgment is sceptical) is the institution of *qetsatsah*, 'severance', whose 'precise import', Daube remarked in 1955, 'has never been investigated'. Thus, we read in the Palestinian Talmud:

When a man sold his ancestral estate, the members of his family brought casks, filled them with parched grain and nuts, and broke them before the children; and the children collected them and said: 'X has been cut off from his estate.' When he reacquired his estate, they did the same, and said: 'X

---

[12] On this reading, and the interpretation of the use of a *shtar* in this context, see further Jackson (note 3), 123f.
[13] Noted but not discussed by Yaron (note 8), 44 n.1.
[14] On the reading here — possibly a loan word for *legatum* — see Jackson (note 3), 125.
[15] Daube, *New Testament Judaism* (note 4), 813.

has returned to his estate.'[16]

Daube's hint was taken up (inter alia) by K. H. Rengstorf, who argued for its relevance to the parable. Rengstorf saw *qetsatsah* as a public ceremony of severance of personal and material relations with the clan (*Sippe*) with whom the individual had come into 'incurable conflict',[17] and accepted that it was designed particularly for its deterrent[18] and pedagogic[19] effect in relation to behaviour which was permitted but socially disapproved.[20] He was particularly impressed by the reversibility of the institution, which he saw as reflected in the 're-investiture' of the prodigal son, and his 'complete restitution ... to his former position of heir, including all rights and duties connected therewith.'[21] However, as Yaron argues,[22] there is no statement that *qetsatsah* entails disinheritance; indeed, reacquisition of the estate is regarded in the *qetsatsah* sources as the normal/desirable sequel. Moreover, there is no parallel in the *qetsatsah* ceremony to the restoration to the son of his former garment and the giving of the ring and shoes,[23] all of which are stressed by Rengstorf as

---

[16] *Jerusalem Kiddushin* 1.5 (translation of Yaron (note 8), 42); the passage notes the use of the same ceremonies when a man married a woman unworthy of him and then subsequently divorced her: see further Jackson (note 3), 127. See also *Jerusalem Talmud Ketubbot* 2:10, *Babylonian Talmud Ketubbot* 28b.

[17] K. H. Rengstorf, *Die Re-Investitur des Verlorenen Sohnes in der Gleichniserzählung Jesu Luk. 15, 11–32* [*Veröffentlichungen der Arbeitsgemeinschaft für Forschung des Landes Nordrhein-Westfalen. Geisteswissenschaften*, 137] (Cologne 1967), 21–27, 70. See also J. D. M. Derrett, 'The Parable of the Prodigal Son', *New Testament Studies*, 14 (1967), 56–74, reprinted in J. D. M. Derrett, *Law in the New Testament* (London 1970), 100–25, reviewing Rengstorf's argument (id., 115f.) but finding it inapplicable to the parable, on the grounds that there is no suggestion in the latter that the prodigal was originally penalised or ostracised by his family.

[18] Rengstorf (note 17), 23.

[19] Id., 24, referring to the role of children in the ceremony.

[20] Cf. M. Katz, *Talmud Yerushalmi Masekhet Kiddushin Perek Rishon* (Ph.D. thesis, Bar-Ilan University, 2004), 130f., concluding that *qetsatsah* was an early social custom, with no halakhic significance for property relations.

[21] Rengstorf (note 17), 71; cf. id., 50f.

[22] Yaron (note 8), 42.

[23] Rengstorf (note 17), 71 (cf. id., 28f., 45–50), argues that the shoes were 'a legal symbol ... connected with the right of tenure'. This is based on the reference to a shoe ceremony in *Midrash Rabbah on Ruth* 4:7 (vii.11), quoted in note 24 below, and see further Jackson (note 3), 129f. (including

indicating the prodigal's complete (and immediate) restoration to his position as heir. On the other hand, there is evidence of shoe ceremonies as an early form of property acquisition,[24] though whether this is the import in the prodigal narrative is far from clear.

the use made by Kenneth Bailey of this source). On Rengstorf's use at 25f. of *Tosefta Baba Batra* 2:5 and *Baba Batra* 52a, see Jackson (note 3), 121 n.30.

[24] *Midrash Rabbah on Ruth* 4:7 (vii.11): 'Formerly they used to acquire the title to a purchase by means of a shoe or sandal, as it is said, A MAN DREW OFF HIS SHOE, but later they acquired the title by means of *qetsatsah*.' While the presentation of *qetsatsah* as a form of *qinyan* is highly questionable (see further Jackson (note 3), 130), the proof text for the shoe ceremony as a form of *qinyan* is Ruth 4:7: 'Thus formerly it was done in Israel in cases of redemption and exchange: to validate any transaction, one man would take off his sandal and hand it to the other. This was the practice in Israel.' There has been much discussion of the relationship of the shoe ceremony in Ruth to that in the *ḥalitsah* ceremony in Deut 25:8–9:

> ... and if he persists, saying, 'I do not wish to take her', then his brother's wife shall go up to him in the presence of the elders, and pull his sandal off his foot, and spit in his face; and she shall answer and say, 'So shall it be done to the man who does not build up his brother's house.'

In a forthcoming study, I take the shoe ceremony in Ruth 4:8 to be performed by Boaz rather than the (unnamed) redeemer, and the *ḥalitsah* ceremony, though undoubtedly involving humiliation (cf. D. Daube, 'The Culture of Deuteronomy', *Orita*, 3 (1969), 27–52, reprinted in C. Carmichael, ed., *Biblical Law and Literature* [*Collected Works of David Daube*, 3] (Berkeley 2003), 995-1013, at 1001–1003; C. M. Carmichael, 'A Ceremonial Crux: Removing a Man's Sandal as a Female Gesture of Contempt', *Journal of Biblical Literature*, 96 (1977), 321–36, at 333–34), to be essentially talionic: the levir ought to have acquired (his deceased brother's wife and estate) by a shoe ceremony; on his failure to perform it, the ceremony is performed *on him*. We may note that the very next paragraph, that of the 'immodest woman wrestler' (so L. Eslinger, 'The Case of the Immodest Lady Wrestler in Deuteronomy XXV 11–12', *Vetus Testamentum*, 31 (1981), 269–81), is overtly talionic.

In this context, we may recall Daube's brilliant account of the interplay of levirate and redemption in the Ruth narrative, as part of the trick played by Boaz on the kinsman: he led him to assume that the woman he had to marry to redeem the estate was Naomi, who would not be able to provide more than (at most) a single son (who would then stand in the place of Avimelekh), but when the redeemer refused and Boaz acquired, Boaz revealed that the levirate widow was in fact Ruth (whom Naomi had set up to be an *ersatz* widow of Elimelekh, in order to persuade Boaz, who had himself initially been reluctant when he too thought it was Naomi). See D. Daube, *Ancient Jewish Law* (Leiden 1981), 37–43, reprinted in C. Carmichael, ed., *New Testament Judaism* [*Collected Works of David Daube*, 2] (Berkeley 2000), 492–99; cf. now D. Daube, *The Deed and the Doer in the Bible. David Daube's Gifford Lectures, Volume 1*, ed. C. Carmichael (West Conshohocken, PA, 2008), 204–207.

Yet there remains an element of (deliberate) ambiguity in the situation, whatever the background rules on the effect of both the *matanat bari* and the 'advance', revolving around the effective reversibility by the father of both the original division and whatever new arrangements are made on the prodigal's return. For even if the prodigal is indeed fully entitled ultimately to take his share in any property acquired by the father after the original division (the mishnaic view), there was nothing to prevent the father from giving a further *matanat bari* to the older son: this indeed may be what he hints at doing when he says: 'all that is mine is yours'. And that may not be the end of the matter, since any such second *matanat bari* would also not apply to subsequently-acquired property, though the latter might also be redirected to the older son by making an appropriate *shekhiv mera* once the father was on his deathbed. And if, conversely, the prodigal returned *without* any existing legal right to share, either immediately or on his father's death, in property acquired since the original division, the older son might well fear that his father would later exercise his right to reinstate him. The older son's reaction, as has been widely noted, is not recorded, and this is sometimes taken to imply that he remained unimpressed. We can understand his cynicism, whichever version of the law we adopt. A family arrangement which had originally appeared, with the prodigal's departure, clear, has now become, with his return, an unresolved problem (a Rumsfeldian 'known unknown').

We should hardly be surprised at the legal ambiguity. It reflects an issue I find increasingly important for our understanding of the early history of Jewish law: the process of institutionalisation, or the transformation of social (often 'self-executing'[25]) rules into legal rules. If we go back to the

---

[25] B. S. Jackson, *Wisdom-Laws: A Study of the Mishpatim of Exodus 21:1–22:16* (Oxford 2006), esp. 23–39 and chapter XIII; B. S. Jackson, 'Marriage and Divorce: From Social Institution to Halakhic Norms', in C. Hempel, ed., *The Dead Sea Scrolls. Texts and Context* (Leiden 2010) (forthcoming). Though Daube was fairly traditional in his assumptions about the institutionalisation of the legal system in biblical times, he made pioneering and enduring observations on the processes of linguistic institutionalisation (and their implications) in his accounts of the relationship between the verb and the action noun derived from it. Thus in

disposition of Abraham's estate in Genesis 25, the issue is surely not whether there was already a legal rule that, by sending away the children of the concubines with gifts, the patriarch was thereby disinheriting them. Comparison may be made with the disinheritance of Jephthah.²⁶ What mattered was simply the patriarch's intention in making the gift. Was the position of the father in the parable any different? Could he not change his mind regarding the effect of the original 'advance'? Yaron seeks to juridify the issue by arguing that it was possible to insert within an advance a clause excluding from the ultimate inheritance, thus modifying the rule in the Mishnah:

> In the absence of a duty of collation it would be important to know whether a certain gift was meant to be in addition to the son's legal share or as compensation. In each case the wording of the disposition would have to be investigated, and if, as might happen, the wording was not clear, this would give rise to doubts and litigation.²⁷

But the text of the parable provides no clue (other than the subsequent behaviour of the participants in the story) as to whether this was assumed to have been done; indeed, there is no suggestion in the text that the 'advance' was incorporated in a written document. In fact, the prodigal's language on greeting his father (encouraged, no doubt, by the father's affectionate embrace) may perhaps imply a claim (not necessarily sincere) that he did retain a legal entitlement, which he was prepared to renounce on moral grounds: 'I am no longer worthy (οὐκέτι εἰμὶ ἄξιος) to be called your son', vs. 21.

Of course, the use of a clause in a document of gift stating its effect on the ultimate distribution may be regarded as a

---

D. Daube, *Roman Law. Linguistic, Social and Philosophical Aspects* (Edinburgh 1969), 11, he observed: 'To put it at its lowest, there has been some reflection on the activity in question, there is some trend towards abstraction, systematization, classification perhaps, the thing is becoming more of an institution.' See further (with examples) B. S. Jackson, 'Legal Drafting in the Ancient Near East in the Light of Modern Theories of Cognitive Development', *Mélanges à la mémoire de Marcel-Henri Prévost* (Paris 1982), 60f.

²⁶ Judges 11:1–7, where disinheritance is described in the same terms, 'hatred' (*sin'ah*) and 'driving out' (*garash*), as commonly in divorce.

²⁷ Yaron (note 8), 45.

survival of a wider and less formal (pre-institutional) discretion inherent in the father's act of will.[28] Daube points to another form in which the father's will may effectively disinherit the recipient of an 'advance', notwithstanding the mishnaic rule: a vow interdicting the son from the use of the property (*qonam*)[29] — but there is no suggestion of any such vow in the parable.

In short, the position of the returning prodigal remains an 'unresolved problem'.[30] I take this to be deliberate. For it corresponds to the message of the theological and referential levels of the parable, to which I now turn.

Was the returning prodigal sincere in his confession and repentance? The narrator comes close to implying that he was not: the prodigal is depicted in vss. 17–19 as calculating that if he goes home to his father, and confesses his sin (a crucial part of the Jewish concept of *teshuvah*), then he will at least be taken back into the home, and receive basic support. Nor does the context of the parable in Luke speak unambiguously for a sincere repentance. The parable follows immediately on two shorter parables, all of them designed to justify to the Pharisees Jesus' consorting (and eating) with 'tax collectors and sinners'.[31] But neither a lost and found sheep nor a lost and found coin is the strongest metaphor for a sincere penitent.

On the other hand, when we reach the parable of the prodigal, that issue does arise: even if the prodigal arrived home as a calculating, insincere penitent, that does not exclude the possibility that the father — who, as has been noted,[32] makes no attempt at all to *test* the returnee's sincerity — *immediately* forgives him, anticipating that

---

[28] Rengstorf is sensitive to the issue, but ambiguous in his conclusions. On the one hand, the restitution of the prodigal is 'an authentic legal act' which effects a 'complete restitution ... to his former position of heir, including all rights and duties connected therewith'. Rengstorf (note 17), 71; cf. id., 50f. On the other hand, he stresses (at id., 23 n.46) the informal nature of the institution, and at id., 26, characterises it as a usage with legal consequences, rather than a *Rechtsakt* in the strict sense.

[29] Daube (note 4), 813.

[30] As in the title of my full account of the issue: note 3, above.

[31] Nor are we told that the sinners and tax collectors actually repented before (or when) Jesus received and ate with them.

[32] B. B. Scott, *Hear Then the Parable* (Minneapolis, MN, 1989), 117.

ultimately, and partly as a result of his very reintegration within the family, he will indeed sincerely repent of his previous misdoings.

In fact, Jewish thought supports the view that repentance is a process rather than an event. Philo notes that parents often 'do not lose thought for their wastrel (ἀσώτων) children but ... lavish their kindness on the wastrels more than on the well behaved .... In the same way, God too ... takes thought also for those who live a misspent life, thereby giving them *time for reformation*, and also keeping within the bounds His own merciful nature ....'[33] The following late *midrash*[34] has been cited[35] as a parallel to the reception given by the father to the returning prodigal:

A king had a son who had gone astray from his father a journey of hundred days; his friends said to him, 'Return to your father'; he said, 'I cannot'. Then his father sent to say, 'Return as far as you can, and I will come to you the rest of the way.' So God says, 'Return to me, and I will return to you.'

In short, the penitential status of the returning prodigal is itself an 'unresolved problem': he is given an initial benefit of the doubt, and time to prove himself. And on that, we may assume, will depend the ultimate destination of the father's residual estate.

This theme, I would suggest, also informs the third ('referential') level of the parable. Nothing in the preceding argument turns upon the fact that the prodigal is the younger brother. But we cannot ignore that fact, or the significance of its obvious intertextualities with the Hebrew Bible,[36] where we encounter some complex interactions between law, social practice, narrative and covenantal promise. Deuteronomy

---

[33] Philo, *De providentia* 2.4–6; F. H. Colson, trans., *Philo*, 9 [Loeb Classical Library] (London 1960), ad loc. (emphasis supplied). I am indebted to Gerald Downing for drawing my attention to this passage.

[34] *Pesikta Rabbati* 184b–185a.

[35] By Scott (note 32), 117, from C. G. Montefiore and H. Loewe, *A Rabbinic Anthology* (London 1938), 321.

[36] For a wider-ranging (perhaps too wide-ranging) account of intertextualities with the younger brother theme, see Derrett, *Law in the New Testament* (note 17), 116–19. On the theme in the Hebrew Bible and the ancient Near East, see above all F. E. Greenspahn, *When Brothers Dwell Together. The Preeminence of Younger Siblings in the Hebrew Bible* (New York and Oxford 1994).

21:15–17 presupposes the basic institution of primogeniture, and addresses a possible problem in its application:

> If a man has two wives, the one loved and the other disliked, and they have borne him children, both the loved and the disliked, and if the first-born son is hers that is disliked, then on the day when he assigns his possessions as an inheritance to his sons, he may not treat the son of the loved as the first-born in preference to the son of the disliked, who is the first-born, but he shall acknowledge the first-born, the son of the disliked, by giving him a double portion of all that he has, for he is the first issue of his strength; the right of the first-born is his.

The main concern here is very specific: if a man wants to discriminate against his oldest son by not giving him the double portion (which clearly he is legally entitled to do), he should not so discriminate *merely* because he has a (relative) dislike for the mother of the older son, as against the mother of the son he chooses to prefer. The practice (or possibility) against which Deuteronomy protests is in fact exactly what Jacob did (as Carmichael has, to a large extent, maintained[37]): in Genesis 49:2–4, he refuses to give the 'birthright' to Reuven, his oldest son, the son of the non-preferred Leah; instead, he gives what amounts to a double portion[38] to Joseph, the son of the preferred wife, Rachel. He does this by adopting the two sons of Joseph, Ephraim and Menasseh,[39] and giving them portions along with Joseph's brothers instead of Joseph. Thus, Ephraim and Menasseh appear as two of the twelve tribes of Israel, taking the place of Joseph. This is exactly the way in which the 'double portion' is conceived to operate, as it is spelled out in later Rabbinic sources. But Jacob has applied it to the benefit of a son who is not the oldest, but whose mother was preferred to that of the oldest.

---

[37] C. M. Carmichael, 'Uncovering a Major Source of Mosaic Law: The Evidence of Deut 21:15-2:5', *Journal of Biblical Literature*, 101/4 (1982), 505–20.

[38] Cf. J. H. Hertz, *The Pentateuch and Haftorahs. Genesis* (London 1929), 397 (on Gen 48:5); G. N. Knoppers, 'The Preferential Status of the Eldest Son Revoked?', in S. L. McKenzie and T. Römer, eds., *Rethinking the Foundations. Historiography in the Ancient World and in the Bible. Essays in Honour of John Van Seters* (Berlin and New York 2000), 119.

[39] Gen 48:5: 'Ephraim and Menasseh shall be mine, as Reuben and Simeon are.'

Of course, this is not the only example of the preference of a younger son to an older son in the patriarchal narratives;[40] Isaac is preferred to Ishmael, Jacob to Esau. There is, however, a vital difference in the operation of this preference between the successions to Abraham and Isaac on the one hand, Jacob on the other. In the two former cases, the older son (Ishmael, Esau) is excluded *entirely*. In the latter, the older son receives a 'normal' share in the inheritance; he is excluded only from the 'double portion'. This is important for our understanding of the parable of the prodigal son, since it is the succession to Jacob, and particularly the role of Joseph in that narrative, which it evokes.

The principal intertextualities of Luke's prodigal, in my view,[41] are with the story of Joseph,[42] and not simply as a younger brother who was lost to his family — as a result, at least in part, of his own arrogance and overweening behaviour — but who later (after attaching himself to a rich foreigner in the context of a famine) was found and restored (albeit that the material relations between this lost son and his family turn out to be the reverse of those in the New Testament). In Luke, the first thing which the father orders done, on the return of the prodigal, is: 'Bring quickly the best robe' — an allusion, perhaps, to Joseph's 'coat of many

---

[40] This phenomenon has been well noted in the literature, as is reflected in the titles of the monographs of both Greenspahn (note 36), and R. Syren, *The Forsaken Firstborn: A Study of a Recurrent Motif in the Patriarchal Narratives* (Sheffield 1993).

[41] *Aliter*, K. E. Bailey, *Jacob & the Prodigal: How Jesus Retold Israel's Story* (Downers Grove, IL, 2003), 121–94, who argues for parallels with the story of Jacob's exile and return in Gen 27:1 – 36:8: Isaac unintentionally gives Jacob his 'primary blessing', whereupon Jacob has to flee to a 'far country'; on his return, he (eventually) revisits Isaac, after which Isaac dies and Esau, the older brother, departs. Many (but not all) of Bailey's parallels on matters of detail are worthy of study. We are not, of course, required, for these purposes, to limit ourselves to a single narrative as a source of intertextuality. Nevertheless, the difference between the excluded Esau and the non-excluded older brother of the parable is surely significant for the underlying theological message.

[42] Cf. M. D. Goulder, *Luke. A New Paradigm*, 2 (Sheffield 1989), 611f. Other aspects are stressed by Derrett, *Law in the New Testament* (note 17), 120: 'He was virtually exchanged for sandals, so the mention of sandals is appropriate. The rejoicing of the father resembles that of Joseph himself and of his own father.'

colours',[43] which itself has been seen as a leadership symbol.[44] For we may recall that in Genesis 37:3 the observation that 'Now Israel loved Joseph more than any other of his children, because he was the son of his old age' immediately precedes the notice that Jacob himself made the coat for him. Moreover, Joseph certainly was, in the eyes of Jacob, first (shown to be) dead, and then restored to life.[45] Indeed, the first thing that Joseph does, when presented with his youngest brother, Benjamin, is to order the slaughter of animals for a feast (Genesis 43:16). And Joseph, the younger son, did, as we have seen, ultimately receive the 'double portion'.

Against this background, we may argue that the relationship between the older brother and the prodigal son is intended to convey a message about the relationship between historic Israel and the new church.[46] For it would not have been necessary to introduce the theme of sibling rivalry in order to generate a parable concerned merely with the jealousy of the righteous at the religious re-integration of sinners. The prodigal, on this reading, is indeed in line (despite the father's reassurances to his older brother) to receive what we may non-technically describe as a 'double portion' — both the original advance and his ultimate (possible) share in the distribution of the father's after-acquired property.

How, then, does the parable conceive of the relationship between historic Israel and the new church? It certainly falls short of both supersessionism[47] and triumphalism. It seems

---

[43] Cf. Derrett, *Law in the New Testament* (note 17), 118, who adds the ring (taken to be a signet ring) as a parallel. On this, see further Jackson (note 3), 128 n.59.

[44] Hertz (note 38), 310 (supporting the translation from the LXX, Targum Yonatan and Kimchi): 'We now know from the painted Tombs of the Bene Hassain in Egypt that, in the Patriarchal age, Semitic chiefs wore coats of many colours as insignia of rulership.'

[45] Gen 37:31–33, which Daube (*Studies in Biblical Law* (Cambridge 1947), 4–5, 8–10) showed to reflect the law of the shepherd proving the loss of a sheep to a wild animal by displaying its carcass: Exod 22:12.

[46] Derrett, *Law in the New Testament* (note 17), 119, observes that the Church saw the younger brothers of Jewish biblical history as 'types' of Jesus.

[47] Cf. F. G. Downing's interpretation of Luke's attitude to the law in 'Law and Custom: Luke-Acts and late Hellenism', in B. Lindars, ed., *Law and Religion. Essays on the Place of the Law in Israel and Early Christianity*

to proclaim a pluralist message:[48] the father may indeed seek to reassure his older son that his merited, privileged position is not threatened, while at the same time extending love and welcome to the sinner. Recall that the stated aspiration of the prodigal son, in deciding to come home, was only to be treated 'as one of your hired servants' (though he is not recorded as having repeated that when he actually met his father). Perhaps, then, the father's approach to the not-yet penitent sinner[49] is pragmatic: we will take him in, and see how he gets on; only if later he is seen genuinely to repent will he actually inherit a share of the Kingdom?[50] Perhaps, indeed, this is a response to *Christian* Pharisees, who maintain that conversion requires circumcision.[51] Luke offers a diplomatic pause[52] in an unresolved problem: let us not alienate converts by radical demands, but let us see how they get on and decide later whether they are to be fully integrated as successors to the covenantal promise. Such an approach certainly entails no rejection of the older brother — or those he is taken to represent.[53]

David Daube's uniqueness lay in the questions and issues he identified, and the creative solutions he proposed to them. He did not always offer definitive proof for his hypotheses, or

---

(Cambridge 1988), 148–58. *Aliter* J. T. Sanders, *The Jews in Luke-Acts* (London 1987), 317, 319, on which see further Jackson (note 3), 144.

[48] Cf. K. E. Bailey, *Finding the Lost. Cultural Keys to Luke 15* (St Louis, MO, 1992), 189, 192.

[49] Bailey (note 48), 148, and Bailey (note 41), 111, maintains that the point of the parable is that Jesus, like the father in the parable, goes out of his way to seek to induce sinners to repent, by receiving them and planning to eat with them.

[50] Derrett, *Law in the New Testament* (note 17), 114 (and see references in n.4) notes a retelling of the story of the prodigal son by Buddhist scholars a century or more afterwards, in which the prodigal is carefully tested to know whether he is fit to enjoy the wealth he can claim.

[51] Acts 15:5: 'But some believers who belonged to the party of the Pharisees rose up, and said, "It is necessary to circumcise them, and to charge them to keep the law of Moses".'

[52] Contrary to the view of some New Testament scholars, who emphasise the prodigal's (immediate) restoration (and its supersessionist meaning), and seek to delete the father's 'and all that is mine is yours' as secondary, or impose on it some metaphorical meaning.

[53] Cf. J. J. O'Rourke, 'Some Notes on Luke xv.11-32', *New Testament Studies*, 18 (1972), 433, concluding: 'One should note that the Lukan parable states that the elder son has a special relationship to the father; thus the anti-Pharisaic or anti-Jewish overtones are not strong.'

systematically pursue their implications. In his supervision of doctoral students, he sought to identify and fortify the particular strengths of each individual, rather than impose on them a single model of scholarship. This study has sought to supplement Daube's insights on the Lukan parable, in a way which draws upon the diversity of approaches which he fostered amongst his students.

VI

David's Teaching in Aberdeen

William M. Gordon*

This contribution gives a brief account of the author's experience of David Daube's teaching in the classes of Roman Law and Jurisprudence in the author's first year of law studies in Aberdeen, and of his teaching of Advanced Roman Law in subsequent years, together with an appreciation of his qualities as a teacher.

Some of those present at the conference had the privilege of preparing a doctoral dissertation under David's supervision and were his pupils in that special sense. It is a sense in which Peter Birks appears to have used the term 'pupil' when reflecting on the position of Roman law in twentieth-century Britain in his contribution on that topic in *Jurists Uprooted*.[1] In connection with Glasgow and the tenure of chairs by David's pupils he mentions only Alan Watson's tenure of the chair of Civil Law, omitting, rather surprisingly in view of his own relationship with him, the fact that Tony Thomas had also held that chair — but an omission explicable if one accepts the special definition of 'pupil'. It seems that I also did not qualify for mention as my own doctoral studies were, as it were, at second hand under the supervision of Peter Stein — himself one of David's distinguished pupils. The nearest that I came in respect of doctoral studies was in

---

* Douglas Professor of Civil Law Emeritus, University of Glasgow.
[1] See J. Beatson and R. Zimmermann, eds., *Jurists Uprooted: German-Speaking Émigré Lawyers in Twentieth-Century Britain* (Oxford 2004), 251.

having David as one of the external examiners of my thesis. Nevertheless I can claim to be a pupil in another more modest sense in that I was one of his first pupils in the classes of Roman Law and Jurisprudence when he came to Aberdeen. I had always thought that our classes, those of 1952–1953, were the first that he taught but I seem to be mistaken in that, as he gave his inaugural lecture on 30 April 1951.[2] However I did attend in 1952 and in subsequent years I attended the Advanced Class in Roman Law which he introduced. In the first year of the Advanced Class I *was* the Advanced class so far as undergraduate students are concerned (although Peter Stein, then a lecturer in the department was also present). The idea of a class of one must seem anathema in universities now conceived rather as profit centres than as seats of learning but it has to be said that as the Ordinary Class was only about a dozen in number an Advanced Class of one following it was quite a respectable percentage. The numbers of students also doubled in the following year when I was joined by Reuven Yaron, then a graduate student pursuing his doctoral studies under David's supervision; such is the power of numbers and percentages as a measure of success. I do of course regret, with all respect to Peter Stein, that I never had the privilege of enjoying supervision by David — although those who did experience it seem also to have found it somewhat terrifying — but I did enjoy his teaching and feel almost as much connected to him as those who were pupils in the narrower sense.

The move to Aberdeen must have been in some degree a culture shock to David, in an academic and perhaps in other senses too. At that time the LL.B. degree had a fairly fixed curriculum, prescribed by ordinance and common to all four ancient Scottish universities. Two components were the classes of Roman or Civil Law, and Jurisprudence, each I think to have 80 lectures over the year. They were taken in the first year of the LL.B. in Aberdeen but because many students took a combined M.A. and LL.B., both as Ordinary

---

[2] 'The Scales of Justice', published in *Juridical Review*, 63 (1951), 109, republished in D. Daube, *Collected Studies in Roman Law*, ed. D. Cohen and D. Simon (Frankfurt am Main 1991), 447.

degrees — there was as yet no Honours degree in law — this first year would have been their third year of university studies. For those taking the B.L. degree it would have been their first year. Most students were part-time as they were also apprenticed to a legal firm and studying law with a view to practice of the profession and in turn mostly with a view to practice as solicitors. Relatively few went to the Bar in Edinburgh from Aberdeen. The system worked well enough at least in principle if the main object of legal education was to produce competent practitioners although it was not conducive to the cultivation of legal scholarship. In most universities teaching law the classes were early in the morning and again in the early evening but in Aberdeen at the insistence of Tom Smith all classes were at the more comfortable hours from 9 a.m. to 1 p.m. This arrangement was not entirely popular with apprentice masters who thought that they were losing valuable apprentice time — valuable to them, that is, as apprentices were then normally paid somewhere between £50 and £100 a year — but it was accepted and it made advanced classes possible. That in turn prepared the way for Honours teaching.

Again most members of staff were part-time, usually solicitors in practice, although that tradition was changing with some prospect of a full-time law degree more on the pattern of the Arts degree. Tom Smith was already there as professor of Scots Law in succession to Sir Thomas Taylor, the then Principal, who was clearly sympathetic to the Law Faculty, and Sandy Anton was appointed to teach Public and Private International Law full-time. Joan Smith, who later became secretary to the Bank of Scotland, also taught Constitutional Law and some Mercantile Law as a full-time lecturer, newly appointed. For Aberdeen it was a very promising start but it was no doubt a rather different atmosphere from that in Cambridge.

One potential problem for David was that his chair was a newly-established chair of Jurisprudence, not Roman or Civil Law. I suppose that David was appointed primarily in view of his distinction as a Romanist. Presumably he had never given a course of lectures on jurisprudence in the sense of legal philosophy and legal concepts, as was expected for the prescribed 80 lectures, although his capacity to do so cannot be in doubt. I learned from Peter Stein that he solved the problem for legal philosophy in a pragmatic way by basing himself on a work by an eminent scholar, an opponent of positivist legal philosophy, with whose views he found himself, understandably, much in sympathy. I refer to Helmut Coing, whose *Grundzüge der Rechtsphilosophie* he more or less translated. Perhaps he learned from his parttime colleagues, one of whom taught Procedure and Evidence openly from the prescribed text-books, embellished it has to be said, from his own extensive experience of practice. It was also a practice not unknown elsewhere although not necessarily with the same openness or with the same possible excuse of lack of time for preparation. At any rate David was unlikely to be detected and would perhaps have enjoyed the joke if he had been; he certainly had a mischievous side and it must be said that his model was well-chosen as no doubt were the models of others. It is interesting that he referred to Coing's book at the beginning of his inaugural lecture and in the course of it he did also refer to both G. W. Paton's *Textbook of Jurisprudence* and W. Friedmann's *Legal Theory*, the books which were the prescribed textbooks for the Jurisprudence course. However that may be, what was detectable even to the novices to whom he was lecturing was that he adopted an entirely different style from the lectures which he delivered to the class of Roman Law.

In the Roman Law class he used to appear with a couple of sheets of paper on which there seemed to be typed at most a couple of lines of text. Commonly he used only one sheet for a lecture although he might sometimes move on to a second one in the course of the lecture but he cannot have had more than a few headings to guide him and he took his time in his exposition. He might have been following the advice first to tell students what you are going to say, then say it and then tell them what you have said. He seemed to enjoy the lectures as much as his students did. In the class of Jurisprudence he came in with a fairly thick wad of notes closely typed. He delivered his lectures at some speed and one had the sense of a performance of duty rather than enjoyment, which it is now easier to understand if he was in effect reading from a prepared text. Maybe he also wished to get home for lunch because the lectures were from 12 noon to 1 p.m. Whether this changed in his later years in Aberdeen once he had had greater experience I do not know, of course, but he did return to what we thought of as his normal style when discussing legal concepts towards the end of the course, by which time he would have had more time for preparation and less need for a systematic treatment. One memory of the class examination is that he had apparently failed to explain sufficiently clearly the contribution of Marx to legal philosophy, as one student referred to Marx as 'Marx the great Russian capitalist' — a description which David read out with some glee, without identifying the culprit, when returning the papers. Another memory which comes to mind from reading his *Jottings*[3] is the statement of his views on the Nuremberg Trials but whether this was in relation to justice in the Jurisprudence lectures or in relation to retroactive legislation in Roman law I am no longer sure. At the time I found his views surprising at first but that shows the force of propaganda and my own naiveté and how little I really knew him then. He made, as always, a powerful and convincing case against the proceedings to open my eyes.

Roman law was really his subject and he was both an attractive personality and an attractive teacher of his subject. There it seems that he could be more himself and I was certainly not alone in enjoying the subject as he taught it. There is no doubt that he was the best teacher that we had in Aberdeen and that in competition with Tom Smith who had, of course, a certain pomposity which contrasted strongly with David's apparent modesty of demeanour, not to mention an accent which was as different as David's from what we were accustomed to hear. I cannot say that David attracted me into the subject as such because I was already attracted to it partly because I had enjoyed the study of Latin both at school and at university and partly because I believed that Roman

---

[3] C. Carmichael, ed., *The Jottings of David Daube* (New York 2008), 12–15.

law was the foundation of Scots law which was to be the main object of study. Time has taught me both that this belief was not entirely justified[4] and that in any case the Roman law that David Daube taught and studied was not quite the Roman law which has influenced Scots law. In fact when I once indicated my interest in the later life of Roman law David made quite clear to me that to pursue that interest involved a whole new field of study and gave me to understand that it was not one that attracted him. Despite the breadth of his scholarship he had enough to do and knew where to draw the line. Perhaps it was as well that Peter Stein became my supervisor when I did venture into that field, and discovered just how true it was that I was entering new territory for which my previous study of Roman law had not really prepared me.

In any case David did not treat the class of Roman Law as a preparation for the study of Scots law. Even if he had thought that this was the right approach he was not equipped to take it, at least when he first came to Aberdeen, as he probably did not know much of Scots law despite a couple of references to it in his inaugural lecture. That he would have been open to knowing more can be taken for granted but it is certainly not the sort of approach which would have accorded with his experience of Roman law either in Germany or in Cambridge. In this respect he would have been at odds with Tom Smith who had no great regard for interpolationist study of the texts of Roman law and thought of Roman law in terms of the Civil law and the Civilian tradition. Whether this affected their relations I do not know and whether David would have made any change if he had stayed longer in Aberdeen is a matter of speculation, but my experience of him was that Roman law was to him a subject in itself and was not to be regarded as a preparation for anything else. J. Spencer Muirhead's *Roman Law* was indeed one recommended textbook. This excellent introduction to the subject was prepared mainly for the benefit of students taking the

---

[4] W. M. Gordon, 'The Civil Law in Scotland', *Edinburgh Law Review*, 5 (2001), 1–15, republished in W. M. Gordon, *Roman Law, Scots Law and Legal History* (Edinburgh 2007), 324–39.

examinations of the Law Society of Scotland when that body thought that all solicitors should have some introduction to an important aspect of Scotland's legal history. It did attempt to point out the connections with Scots law, but we were left by David to make our own connections.

Even if from my point of view the course on Roman law was not all that I expected the course itself was anything but a disappointment. David presented his material in good humour — and with humour. He always connected well with his audience and in turn he appreciated awareness of the source of any of the Biblical references which he made from time to time. He always seemed to have a conspiratorial air as if he were revealing important secrets rather than simply expounding the rules of Roman law. A peculiar fascination was the way he manipulated the little device he used to help his breathing and which he invariably kept in the inside pocket of his jacket. He scarcely paused to make use of it, all without any trace of embarrassment. Much more intriguing was his strongly accented English which contrasted strangely with his obvious complete command of the language and all its nuances and peculiarities and his wide knowledge of English literature, but there was the occasional oddity, as when he described a slave-boy as a caddy — clearly out of a golfing context. But one suspected that he knew quite well what he was doing and could have explained and illustrated the wider usage of that term in the eighteenth century. One thing that he particularly seemed to like was to have a standing joke. In the case of the class of Roman Law it was that he claimed that he gained all his news of current affairs from the *Evening Express* (he always stressed the first syllable of 'Express'). He claimed that this and *The Observer* were the only newspapers that he read and no doubt he did read both, the former for its local interest, but the joke was that the *Evening Express* was very much a local newspaper, the sister paper of the Aberdeen *Press and Journal* which then had the reputation of being extremely parochial in its coverage. It was alleged, although the story may be apocryphal — an urban myth nowadays no doubt — that it reported the sinking of the Titanic under the headline

'Maritime Disaster. Aberdeen Man Lost At Sea'. His lectures were therefore always something to look forward to and brighten the day, the more so that they were the first of the day.

What he taught seems in retrospect to have been in general fairly conventional but that may be a trick of memory as I absorbed what he taught as being the way it was without too much awareness of all the controversies among scholars. It is also somewhat difficult to disentangle what I learned as a student from what I later gained from reading his numerous contributions to our understanding of Roman law. We were seldom if ever referred to periodical literature at that time although other views were mentioned and disposed of and we were, reasonably enough in our ignorance, prepared to accept what was so engagingly presented to us as gospel. I have a recollection that Peter Stein once told me that the model for his lectures was probably H. Siber's *Römisches Recht*, which has the fuller title *in Grundzügen für Vorlesungen*, but if this was the model there was no indication that it was treated with the same respect as Coing's *Grundzüge* and I am sure that Buckland must have played a part. What helped to enliven his lectures was his explanations of why the law was as he said it was and how it was likely to have come into being. It was not simply an exposition of the rules but an exposition of the reason for them. Undoubtedly he did incorporate his own views and when he did so, he managed to make them appear so reasonable that they must be right. That I suppose is one of the gifts of a great teacher: to be able to persuade as much by force of personality as by force of argument. Examples that come to mind are his explanation that the meaning of concealment of a neighbour in a contract of sale in the text Digest 18.1.35.8 referred to a problem of boundaries rather than a troublesome person next door,[5] or his well-known views that the thirty days referred to in the third chapter of the *lex Aquilia* meant the thirty days after

---

[5] See D. Daube, 'Three Notes on Digest 18.1, Conclusion of Sale', *Law Quarterly Review*, 73 (1957), 379, republished in *Collected Studies* (note 2), 603.

the injury[6] and that *damnum* meant loss and not damage.[7] We also enjoyed his explanation that the curse *intestatus vivito* uttered in Plautus's play, *Curculio*, could have meant 'live without testicles' rather than 'live intestate' when he was discussing the prevalence or otherwise of intestacy at Rome[8] — I do not seem to remember him saying that it could also mean 'incapable of being called as a witness' — and the tale of Tremellius Scropha and the sow concealed beneath his wife's bed to foil the searchers for it, when he was expounding the law of theft and the liability of someone on whose premises stolen property was found.[9] One valuable observation that has always stuck with me is that certain rules are so much taken for granted that they may never be written down but understanding of the way the law works is distorted if this is not borne in mind.[10]

He used a certain freedom in following the prescribed syllabus. According to it one part of the course was an introduction based on the *Institutes* of Gaius and Justinian. Then there was supposed to be a study of a title of the Digest. That presumably was prescribed with a view to preparing candidates for the Scottish Bar because there was a requirement that they prepare and deliver a lecture on a title of the Digest prescribed by the Faculty of Advocates as part of the public examination which was required as an element of the procedure for admission to the Bar. This requirement had in fact become a pure formality and there was no question of a proper lecture on any title but evidently that was not

---

[6] See D. Daube, 'On the Third Chapter of the *lex Aquilia*', *Law Quarterly Review*, 52 (1936), 253, republished in *Collected Studies* (note 2), 3.

[7] See D. Daube, 'On the Use of the Term *damnum*', in *Studi in onore di Siro Solazzi* (Naples 1948), 93, republished in *Collected Studies* (note 2), 279; cf. 'Nocere and Noxa', *Cambridge Law Journal*, 7 (1939), 23 at 40–41, republished in *Collected Studies* (note 2), 71 at 88–89.

[8] See D. Daube, 'The Preponderance of Intestacy at Rome', *Tulane Law Review*, 39 (1965), 187, republished in *Collected Studies* (note 2), 1087.

[9] See D. Daube, 'Some Comparative Law — *furtum conceptum*', *Tijdschrift voor Rechtsgeschiedenis*, 15 (1937), 48 (not republished in *Collected Studies*).

[10] See D. Daube, 'The Self-Understood in Legal History', *Juridical Review* (n.s.), 18 (1973), 126 (also 'Das Selbstverständliche in der Rechtsgeschichte', *Zeitschrift der Savigny-Stiftung für Rechtsgeschichte* (romanistische Abteilung), 90 (1973), 1), republished in *Collected Studies* (note 2), 1277.

VI. DAVID'S TEACHING IN ABERDEEN

recognised in the university syllabus. However the requirement of the university syllabus, as I recall, was reduced to a couple of special lectures on *iniuria* as either David had run out of time or he realised the impossibility of meeting the requirement of the syllabus adequately according to his standards in the time available. He was never one to be too tied down by rules and regulations as I suppose befits an expert in the dodges that people get or got up to in order to find a way round awkward laws.[11] In those days the syllabus was in any case very general and did not provide a detailed breakdown of the lectures or proposed lectures.

Other memories of the Ordinary Classes were the hospitality offered to the classes in the form of a sherry party at David's home and his approachability. The former was certainly unusual in the austere Northeast and perhaps reflected the influence of Cambridge. Only Tom Smith, accustomed to the ways of Oxford, did likewise. My experience of his willingness to help his students was that he said that he could be consulted on any difficulty and did not mind being telephoned at home if he were not in his room in the former church of St Mary's in Old Aberdeen, where classes were held. I did make the thoughtless mistake at first of phoning him on a Saturday which he, of course, observed as the Jewish Sabbath but when I did make contact he very helpfully explained a difficulty I had over the seller's liability in respect of undisclosed servitudes. It then emerged when I saw the paper for the class examination that he had already set this very question in the examination which gave both of us some amusement when the papers were returned. A friend also who took the class along with me has told me that when he missed the December class examination because of illness David sent him a get-well card.

Another novelty for the time was that we were asked for feedback on the classes. My own reaction was that Jurispru-

---

[11] Cf. D. Daube, 'Dodges and Rackets in Roman Law', summarized in *Proceedings of the Classical Association*, 61 (1964), 28, and 'Fraud No. 3', in N. MacCormick and P. Birks, eds., *The Legal Mind: Essays for Tony Honoré* (Oxford 1986), 1, republished respectively in *Collected Studies* (note 2), 1081 and 1409, and D. Daube, *Roman Law: Linguistic, Social and Philosophical Aspects* (Edinburgh 1968), 92–116.

dence would be better treated in a later year when students had gained more knowledge of the legal system and I think I also suggested a closer connection between Roman and Scots law. The former may have borne fruit but not the latter.

David also thought it appropriate that students be exposed to international scholarship. Probably in his second or third year Wolfgang Kunkel was invited to Aberdeen and lectured to the class. I say that it was probably in David's second or third year that this happened as I remember that Kunkel sat in on one of the sessions of the Advanced Class and I was then the only undergraduate member. This practice is certainly valuable in principle although it may not always be as much appreciated by students as one would wish.

Moving on to the Advanced Class of Roman Law the first thing to mention is the part played by David in the acquisition by Aberdeen of the library of Francis de Zulueta who retired about the time of David's arrival. Without that or a comparable acquisition it would scarcely have been possible to take Roman law beyond the level of the Ordinary Class, as it provided a working research library with all the tools for advanced study, opening up a whole new world of learning. Presumably there was a promise of such a facility to help tempt David to Aberdeen although it could hardly be expected to be, and indeed was not, enough to tempt him to remain when All Souls beckoned all too soon.

I have already mentioned that I was at first the only undergraduate member of the Advanced Class, there in response to his invitation, readily accepted. I was even prepared to sacrifice Public International Law in its favour but I am not sure that I did much more than provide a reason for holding the class. My only companion apart from Peter Stein was the librarian and secretary to the Law Faculty, Mrs MacBean, who took down the lectures in shorthand for David's benefit. In this class it became something of a joke that he invariably started his exposition of a text with the views of Gerhard Beseler, the arch-interpolationist: 'Beseler brackets the following . . . .' The Digest title which he dealt with was 18.1 on sale and he went through it pretty well text-by-text while I tried to follow his acute interpretations. I can recall only one real contribution that I made, while he was discussing Digest 18.1.41: the suggestion that *utiliter agere* might mean 'sue effectively' rather than 'sue with an *actio utilis*', a suggestion that he acknowledged in his article with that title, arguing that the phrase never meant 'to sue with an *actio utilis*'[12] — a thesis curiously like that of many of Beseler's contributions to criticism of the sources. The lectures, however, did become the source of quite a number of articles and perhaps he found an interested audience stimulating. I should be more sympathetic than I have sometimes been to students who worry about examinations more than what they are learning and why, because I can recall some concern about how on earth I could prepare for any examination. Fortunately there were no examinations and all was learning for the sake of it.

Many of those present at the conference would be familiar with the *arbor Daubiana* tracing David's teaching pedigree back to the Glossators in an unbroken line of oral tradition, and I have sometimes thought that his teaching in the Advanced Class had something in common with the method of lecturing of those masters of the *Corpus Iuris*. First put the text in context, then set out the case, then analyse the reasoning and deal with any contradictory texts. The major difference of course is that the Glossators were looking to the present or looking forward and trying to make a system of the mass of material which was to them a fount — almost *the* fount — of legal wisdom. David was looking back and trying to re-discover the ideas and system of the classical jurists that the Compilers had obscured by their editing of the classical texts. In doing so I think he had a sneaking respect for Beseler as a source of ideas although he usually rejected his suggestions as too extreme. He certainly claimed to be more moderate in his attacks on the authenticity of texts. What I did learn, apart from admiration for David's intellect and his subtlety, was how to use the tools of the modern Romanist's trade, two of which, the *Edictum Perpetuum* and the *Palinge-*

---

[12] See D. Daube, 'Utiliter agere', *IURA*, 11 (1960), 69 at 92 n.77, republished in *Collected Studies* (note 2), 923 at 943 n.77 ('He did not convince Mr. W. M. Gordon').

nesia, had been provided by David's own master Otto Lenel, and it was of course David who led me into an academic career.

If I could sum up I would say that from the point of view of the students he was simply incomparable as a teacher. For those focussed on a professional career his impact was perhaps limited as his approach did not offer immediate benefit but they at least carried forward a happy memory of Roman law, as clearly was not the case in other Scottish universities, and they may well have learned more from him than they realised.

VII

Remarks on David Daube's Lectures on Sale, with Special Attention to the *liber homo* and *res extra commercium*

Ernest Metzger[*]

This article discusses a collection of lecture notes on the Roman law of sale prepared by David Daube for an advanced course conducted at the University of Aberdeen from 1954 to 1955. The article considers in detail Daube's lecture on the sale of the liber homo *and* res extra commercium *in Roman law. An excerpt from that lecture is attached as an* Appendix. *His treatment of the subject is unfinished (and unpublished), though it is possible to see how his views might have developed. The final section offers an opinion on Daube's approach to interpreting texts and its value to students.*

David Daube left behind a collection of lecture notes in typescript, prepared for a course in the Roman law of sale. He gave the course at the University of Aberdeen in the academic years 1953/54 and 1954/55. This article discusses the course, and the character and contents of the typescript. It then briefly discusses Daube's treatment of an issue in sale (the sale of the *liber homo* and *res extra commercium*) on which, exceptionally, he did not publish. The final section offers an opinion on Daube's approach to interpreting texts, and suggests that students with no acquaintance of this approach are impoverished.

---

[*] Douglas Professor of Civil Law, University of Glasgow. My thanks to Peter Stein and Jonathan M. Daube for certain details, and especially to William M. Gordon for his frequent assistance.

Ernest Metzger, 'Remarks on David Daube's Lectures on Sale, with Special Attention to the *liber homo* and *res extra commercium*', in E. Metzger, ed., *David Daube: A Centenary Celebration* (Glasgow: Traditio Iuris Romani, 2010), 101–26. Copyright © 2010 by Ernest Metzger (content and typographical arrangement). All rights reserved. ROMANLEGALTRADITION.ORG

This article is intended to complement the remarks of William M. Gordon, also in this volume.[1] Professor Gordon attended the course for which the typescript was prepared, and in fact was the sole undergraduate to attend. He has provided invaluable details to help make sense of this unique document.

What makes it unique? First, though most of the substantive remarks can be found in Daube's published works, the notes themselves are a verbatim record of his teaching. His presentation is less guarded, and his mood more playful, than in his published works. At the same time the notes are nearly as lucid and polished as anything he published. Second, the course itself is of a kind — the examination of a Digest title — that no longer exists in the United Kingdom. The course in fact made philological demands on its audience that are not tolerated today.[2] In this regard the notes are a record of a lost time. Last, Daube recurs frequently to Aberdeen and the University for illustration. This naturally turns the notes into a kind of local document, but less obviously they become more intimate, and a sense of the occasion is stronger.

The course

The course was titled 'Advanced Roman Law' and was announced in the Aberdeen University Calendar a year in advance of first being offered:[3]

---

[1] W. M. Gordon, 'David's Teaching in Aberdeen', in E. Metzger, ed., *David Daube: A Centenary Celebration* (Glasgow 2010), 88–100.

[2] I suspect the last teacher in the United Kingdom to lecture in this style was John Barton, Fellow of Merton College, Oxford, who retired in 1996. He gave a course in Roman *condictiones*, which I attended in the early 1990s.

[3] *The Aberdeen University Calendar for the Year 1952–1953* (Aberdeen 1952), 381. The works recommended are: J. Mackintosh, *The Roman Law of Sale*, 2nd ed. (Edinburgh 1907); F. de Zulueta, *The Roman Law of Sale* (Oxford 1945). De Zulueta's book was amended to meet Daube's criticism on a small point that arose during the lectures (MS 52–53). The issue was the meaning of 'evictum' in D.18.1.8.1 (Pomp. 9 *Sab.*), which Mackintosh (at p. 27) translated as 'wrested' and de Zulueta (at p. 89) translated as 'snatched away'. Daube called these translations 'stupid' (MS 53) and 'strange' ('Purchase of a Prospective Haul', in *Studi in onore di Ugo Enrico Paoli* (Florence 1955), 297). Du Zulueta amended the of-

ADVANCED ROMAN LAW

(*This course will not be available before 1954*)
Selected Title from *the Digest* for Special study. The Title for 1954 will be XVIII, 1, " De Contrahenda Emptione ".
This course is intended to consist of 35 lectures, to be delivered in one term.

Books recommended—
J. Mackintosh, *Roman Law of Sale*; F. de Zulueta, *Roman Law of Sale*.

University Calendar, 1952–1953

To present 35 lectures in a single term was ambitious, particularly as the ten-week term in which the course was scheduled to appear (20 April – 25 June 1954) was foreshortened for examinations:[4]

Third Year

	Winter Term.		
Conveyancing	Professor MacRitchie	Daily 9-10	– –
Comparative Law	Dr. J. Fackenheim	Daily 11-12	3 3
Evidence, Pleading and Procedure	Mr. A. Leslie Hay	Daily 12-1	6 6
	Spring Term		
Conveyancing	Professor MacRitchie	Daily 9-10	– –
International Private Law	Mr. A. E. Anton	Daily 11-12	3 3
Evidence, Pleading and Procedure	Mr. A. Leslie Hay	Daily 12-1	– –
	Summer Term.		
Forensic Medicine	Dr. R. Richards	Daily 8-9	5 5
Public International Law	Mr. A. E. Anton	Daily 11-12	3 3
Comparative Law	Dr. J. Fackenheim	Daily 12-1	– –
Advanced Roman Law	Professor Daube and	(Each twice weekly	– –
Advanced Jurisprudence	Mr. W. P. G. Stein	as may be arranged).	

University Calendar, 1953–1954

The calendar printed for the following academic year (1954–1955) announced the course as it had done previously, but changing 'one term' to 'three terms':[5]

---

fending passages in his 1957 revision, acknowledging Daube's advice in the preface.

[4] *Aberdeen University Calendar 1953–1954* (Aberdeen 1953), 377.
[5] *Aberdeen University Calendar 1954–1955* (Aberdeen 1954), 387.

ADVANCED ROMAN LAW

Selected Title from *the Digest* for Special study. The Title for 1955 will be XVIII, 1, " De Contrahenda Emptione ".
This course is intended to consist of 35 lectures, to be delivered in three terms.

Books recommended—
J. Mackintosh, *Roman Law of Sale*; F. de Zulueta, *Roman Law of Sale*.

University Calendar, 1954–1955

The course was now scheduled to be given over three terms, and fell within the second-year curriculum:

Second Year

CLASS.	LECTURER.	DAYS AND HOURS.	FEE.
Winter Term.			
Accounting (*for Law Students*)	} Mr. J. Grant	Daily 9-10	3 3
Administrative Law	Dr. Joan Smith	M.,T.,W., F.10-11	3 3
Scots Law (Professional Course)	} Professor Smith	T., Th. 12-1 F., 11-12	3 3
Jurisprudence	} Professor Daube and Mr. P. G. Stein	M., W., F. 12-1 Times to be arranged	8 8 8 8
Roman Law (Advanced)			8 8
Spring Term.			
Accounting (*for C.A. Students*)	} Mr. J. Grant	Daily 9-10	6 6
†Mercantile Law	Dr. Joan Smith	Daily 10-11	6 6
Scots Law (Professional Course)	} Professor Smith	T., Th. 12-1 F. 11-12	– –
Jurisprudence	} Professor Daube and Mr. P. G. Stein	M., W., F. 12-1 Times to be arranged	– –
Roman Law (Advanced)			– –
Summer Term.			
*Accounting (*for C.A. Students*)	} Mr. J. Grant	Daily 9-10	– –
Conveyancing	Professor MacRitchie	Daily 9-10	8 8
†Mercantile Law	Dr. Joan Smith	Daily 10-11	– –
Scots Law (Professional Course)	} Professor Smith	M., W., 11-12 T., Th. 12-1	– –
Jurisprudence	} Professor Daube and Mr. P. G. Stein	M., W., F. 12-1 Times to be arranged	– –
Roman Law (Advanced)			– –

University Calendar, 1954–1955

The calendar, however, is not wholly trustworthy as a source for the scheduling of lectures. Calendars were printed well in advance of events. Professor Gordon, moreover, has privately noted that, in view of the small number of participants, the lectures could take place at any convenient time. Professor Gordon's own recollection is that he took the course in his second and third years (1953/54 and 1954/55); that Peter Stein was sometimes in attendance;[6] and that Reuven Yaron[7] attended the course after his arrival in the autumn of 1954. Professor Gordon also recalls that the curriculum was under review during his time as an undergraduate; this would account for the fact that the course moved from the third year to the second. The calendar is also somewhat misleading in suggesting the course was offered twice; Daube did not complete title 18.1 in the first year, and in the second year simply picked up where he had left off.

The course was a traditional examination of a single Digest title and proceeded sequentially by fragment, with frequent departures from the sequence when the topic recalled a fragment further ahead. Some of the issues Daube discussed were already the subjects of published papers,[8] while others would appear later.[9] Judging by the length of

---

[6] Now Regius Professor of Civil Law Emeritus, University of Cambridge. In a letter to Professor Gordon dated 7 March 2009, Professor Stein recalls attending the lectures together with Professor Gordon and Mrs MacBean, the secretary. Daube appears to address Professor Stein here: 'I believe antinomies are not unknown to Scots law or even, with all deference to Mr Stein, to English law.' MS 141. See also note 33 below.

[7] Now Professor Emeritus, Hebrew University of Jerusalem.

[8] See, e.g., D. Daube, 'Actions between paterfamilias and filiusfamilias with peculium castrense', in *Studi in memoria di Emilio Albertario*, 1 (Milan 1950), 435–74; 'The Three Quotations from Homer in Digest 18.1.1.1', *Cambridge Law Journal*, 10 (1949), 213–15. One earlier article discusses fragments that fall in the latter part of title 18.1, and possibly corresponds to portions of the typescript which have not yet been located: D. Daube, 'Generalisations in 18.1, de contrahenda emptione', in *Studi in onore di Vincenzo Arangio-Ruiz*, 1 (Naples 1952), 185–200.

[9] See, e.g., Daube, 'Purchase of a Prospective Haul' (note 3); 'Certainty of Price', in D. Daube, ed., *Studies in the Roman Law of Sale Dedicated to the Memory of Francis de Zulueta* (Oxford 1959), 9–45; 'Money and Justiciability', *Zeitschrift der Savigny-Stiftung für Rechtsgeschichte* (rom. Abt.), 96 (1979), 1–16. One later article possibly corresponds to portions of the typescript which have not yet been located: D. Daube, 'Three Notes on Digest 18.1, Conclusion of Sale', *Law Quarterly Review*, 73 (1957), 379–98.

the written notes, sessions will have lasted two hours. There was an excursus on legacies in Lecture No. 13. The course was not examined.[10]

The typescript

The typescript is titled 'David Daube – Lectures on Sale D. 18.1. 1–24'.[11] It has 154 numbered leaves with typewritten catchwords at the base of each page. It contains about 54,000 words, with occasional handwritten corrections. It is divided into sixteen lectures of somewhat different lengths. Only half of the Digest title is represented in the typescript; the remaining half has not been located. It appears, however, that the remaining half does, or did at one time, exist. In a 1960 article Daube mentions the typescript in these words: 'It might, however, be argued that *utiliter* in our text [D.18.1.41 pr.] reflects the Proculian [position]', with a footnote to the remark: 'As was done by the writer himself in unpublished lectures on Digest 18.1. He did not convince Mr W. M. Gordon.'[12] The discussion to which Daube refers is not found in the typescript that survives.

Daube spoke extemporaneously from brief notes.[13] His words were recorded by the secretary, Mrs MacBean, who then prepared a typescript. The particular typescript we possess is almost certainly a subsequent draft. The presentation is simply too polished for a first draft. The citations are accurate, spelling and punctuation are near perfect, and quotations in Latin are largely free from error. At the same time, the typescript preserves the extemporaneous presentation, e.g.,

> The text as it stands says that if I buy from you an object for the sum you bought the object for . . . or if I buy from you an object for whatever I may have in this box, then the sale is valid, because, although there may be ignorance about the price, the price is in effect certain. *Sorry, I should have*

---

[10] Gordon (note 1), 99.
[11] Notwithstanding the title, the lectures proceed through fragment 25.
[12] D. Daube, 'Utiliter agere', *IURA*, 11 (1960), 92 & n.77.
[13] He refers to these notes at MS 94, 96. See also Gordon (note 1), 91 (mentioning the same practice in Daube's ordinary class).

said that the text explains that the price is certain because the sale is clear; and that there is ignorance rather than true uncertainty.[14]

There are handwritten corrections throughout, but they are minor and sparing and none of them, so far as one can tell, is substantive: Daube improved a handful of expressions and altered the punctuation in small ways. Again, this indicates that the notes had already been closely revised.

Contents

Daube takes up every fragment in the title and considers its meaning and condition carefully. All views are considered. He regularly agrees with Lenel,[15] disagrees with Buckland,[16] and grapples with Beseler. He also regularly solicits William Gordon's views. He expresses his own views freely, but when he is uncertain of a resolution, or an answer completely fails him, he says so. He apologises if he believes his arguments fall short.

He offers a large number of what one would call gnomic statements. They tend to concern the interpretation of texts, the habits of jurists, and the failings of modern scholars. Some are familiar from his published works, though perhaps he expressed himself more freely in making these statements privately. Some examples:

A further point against interpolation. There is here a reference to the veteres — the older jurists, which usually means the pre-classical jurists. If the decision were spurious, there would be no such reference. It cannot be invented. There would be no reason for a post-classical interpolator to bring in the old jurists.[17]

The 'tamen' which I think I have explained very well, is usually emended into 'tantum', 'only'. . . . But as you know I do not like such emendations. They frequently cover up a purposeful interference, a change in law. An emendation is plausible when a word is miswritten which has become unintelligible.[18]

---

[14] MS 38–39 (on D.18.1.7.1 (Ulpian 28 *Sab.*)).
[15] Cf. MS 3: 'Well, now, Lenel — who is always right, but I disagree with him — Lenel held that . . . .'
[16] MS 6: 'I know that whenever I disagree with Buckland I am wrong, but still I disagree.' MS 94: 'This modern construction . . . was never thought of by the Romans. True, you find it in Buckland, and Buckland is always right. But I feel sure the Romans lawyers never took this line.'
[17] MS 38 (on D.18.1.7 pr. (Ulpian 28 *Sab.*)).
[18] MS 123 (on D.18.1.18.1 (Pomp. 9 *Sab.*)).

If one does start crossing out, and you shall see that I shall do so quite soon, one should cross out the general definition and leave the more particular cases in.[19]

All these things are rather conjectural, but it is better to take a view rather than leave everything undecided.[20]

Lawyers faced with a difficult problem are apt to pounce on a minor element of the case, make it the basis of their verdict and leave the problem unanswered.[21]

If you find statements about a simple case tacked onto . . . a complicated case, that does not necessarily mean that the simple case was looked at in the same way before the complicated case came up.[22]

There is also of course a good deal of humour.

Don't be afraid, there are only six texts.[23]

For reasons which are no longer clear to me . . . I prefer the view of Buckland.[24]

Now this text raises an interesting difficulty which has been solved in an admirable way by your present lecturer.[25]

This is a text on which I change my mind every time I look at it, and my changes of mind depend less on rational considerations than on weather conditions or the quality of my breakfast.[26]

In view of some disrespectful smiles I noticed last time when struggling with legacy per vindicationem, I will explain why I tried to evade the issue.[27]

I notice that Zulu — no doubt unwittingly, but Freud would find a subconscious motive behind it — in his book on Sale leaves this 'quia' clause untranslated.[28]

I will adopt the manner of post-classical lawyers and put a number of questions without answering them.[29]

He frequently mentions Aberdeen (both the city and University), and the street on which he lived (Osborne Place), to illustrate a point.

---

[19] MS 21.
[20] MS 22.
[21] MS 87.
[22] MS 116.
[23] MS 97.
[24] MS 16.
[25] MS 2. He is referring to 'The Three Quotations from Homer in Digest 18.1.1.1' (note 8).
[26] MS 83.
[27] MS 111. These disrespectful smiles led to an excursus on legacies in Lecture No. 13.
[28] MS 99 (on D.18.1.16 (Pomp. 9 *Sab.*)). De Zulueta leaves *quia nulla obligatio fuit* untranslated: de Zulueta (note 3), 91.
[29] MS 105.

[Y]ou build on my land with your granite (no brick at Aberdeen).[30]

[The sale-or-hire controversy: if a customer asks a craftsman 'to make a vase', it is plainly a sale.] The question could arise only where I tell him 'now you make a vase which has an ornament in the shape of King's College tower on one side and Marischal College [on] the other' and so on.[31]

[Y]ou would usually be able to distinguish a temple from a private dwelling-house, although nowadays some of the private dwelling houses do look like non-conformist chapels. We have one at the Grammar School end of Osborne Place.[32]

[I]f I think I am buying 65 Osborne Place and you think you are selling me a shed in Salisbury Place,[33] there is dissent as regards the corpus and therefore no sale.[34]

Suppose I have land for part of which the Corporation of Aberdeen offers an enormous price because they want to establish there one of their new and noisy departments, while a poor university professor offers me half the price for it.[35]

I wish to buy from you what you may catch this evening when the Lord Provost, who wishes to be re-elected, is going to distribute largess.[36]

The Sale of the *liber homo* and *res extra commercium*

From the whole of the lectures I have chosen a single topic for closer discussion: the sale of certain things which ostensibly cannot be purchased but nevertheless, in the opinion of the jurists, permitted sale remedies.[37] I have chosen this from

[30] MS 134.
[31] MS 133.
[32] MS 25.
[33] Some gentle humour directed at Peter Stein, who had a house in Salisbury Place, small in comparison to the Daubes' spacious house in Osborne Place. Peter Stein will have been present to enjoy the remark.
[34] MS 56.
[35] MS 43 (on D.19.1.13.24 (Ulpian 32 *ed.*)). When he published on the text in 1959, the case was transferred to Oxford: 'Suppose in selling my property in Cornmarket I wish to preserve the peacefulness of the district. I sell it to an academic institution . . . .' Daube, 'Certainty of Price' (note 9), 30. Also Oxonian: 'Suppose I sell part of my estate to a quiet don at a low price though a noisy government department would be prepared to give far more.' Daube, 'Purchase of a Prospective Haul' (note 3), 205 n.4.
[36] MS 53. A reference, naturally, to the purchase of *missilia*.
[37] MS 21–28. He returns to the subject in Lecture No. 16, though confines himself to the fairly narrow questions raised in D.18.1.22, 24 (Ulpian 28 *Sab.*) and 23 (Paul 5 *Sab.*). For the latest views, see F. Procchi, '"Dolus" e "culpa in contrahendo" nella compravendita. Considerazioni in tema di sinallagma genetico', in L. Garofalo, ed., *La compravendita e l'interdipendenza delle obbligazioni nel diritto Romano*, 1 (Milan 2007), 182–244; A. Trisciuoglio, 'Sinallagma genetico e vendita delle "res extra commercium"', in L. Garofalo, ed., *La compravendita e l'interdipendenza delle*

among other topics because, so far as I am aware, Daube never published on it.³⁸ Daube's arguments, moreover, are different from those offered by other scholars. The notes are set out in full in the Appendix below.³⁹ The topic requires a brief introduction.

The term *res extra commercium* broadly indicates things which are beyond the power of private persons to buy and sell. Bonfante:

There is a distinction in the class of things which relates to whether they are more or less open to private juridical relationships; in general scholars tend to express this distinction with the terms *res in commercio* and *res extra commercium* on the one hand, and *res in patrimonio* and *res extra patrimonium* on the other. Both of these terms are found in the sources: in the jurists of the Digest we find the term *in commercio* or *extra commercium*; Gaius, followed by Justinian's Institutes, uses *in patrimonio*, *extra patrimonium* [G.2.1; J.2.1 pr.]. The former denotes that the thing is open (or not open) to a juridical relationship from the 'dynamic' standpoint; the latter shows, so to speak, the 'static' aspect.⁴⁰

---

obbligazioni nel diritto Romano, 1 (Milan 2007), 277–310; L. Winkel, 'Culpa in contrahendo in Roman Law and Some Modern Dutch Court Decisions', in L. de Ligt, et al., eds., *Viva Vox Iuris Romani: Essays in Honour of Johannes Emil Spruit* (Amsterdam 2002), 149–57; R. Zimmermann, *The Roman Law of Obligations* (Oxford 1996), 241–45; R. Evans-Jones and G. MacCormack, 'The Sale of *res extra commercium* in Roman Law', *Zeitschrift der Savigny-Stiftung für Rechtsgeschichte* (rom. Abt.), 112 (1995), 330–51; R. Evans-Jones, 'The Origins of Justinian's Institutes 3.23.5', *Cambridge Law Journal*, 53 (1994), 473–79. For other views cited below see the following works: B. Biondi, 'La vendita di cose fuori di commercio', in *Studi in onore di Salvatore Riccobono*, 4 (Palermo 1936), 1–56; W. W. Buckland, *The Roman Law of Slavery* (Cambridge 1908); F. Haymann, *Die Haftung des Verkäufers für die Beschaffenheit des Kaufsache*, 1 (Berlin 1912); M. Kaser, 'Vom Begriff des "commercium"', in *Studi in onore di Vincenzo Arangio-Ruiz* (Naples 1953), 131–67; P. Stein, *Fault in the Formation of Contract in Roman Law and Scots Law* (Edinburgh 1958); J. A. C. Thomas, 'The Sale of *res extra commercium*', *Current Legal Problems*, 29 (1976), 136–49; F. de Zulueta, *The Roman Law of Sale* (Oxford 1945; rev. 1957).

38 But see below, notes 59–62 and accompanying text.
39 Below, 119–26.
40 P. Bonfante, *La proprietà* [*Corso di diritto Romano*, 2] (Milan 1966), 13–14:

La distinzione delle cose secondo che sono più or meno suscettibili di rapporti giuridici privati in generale si usa designare dagli interpreti coi termini *res in commercio* e *res extra commercium*, ovvero *res in patrimonio* e *res extra patrimonium*. Entrambe le designazioni hanno base nelle fonti: nei giureconsulti delle Pandette abbiamo la designazione *in commercio* o *extra commercio*: Gaio, e con lui le Istituzioni di Giustiniano, usano *in patrimonio*, *extra patrimonium*. Con la prima

Justinian's well-known rule on the sale of *res extra commercium* mentions *loca sacra, relgiosa,* and *publica*,[41] and allows the unknowing buyer of these places to have an action on the sale.

J.3.23.5. Loca sacra vel religiosa, item publica, veluti forum basilicam, frustra quis sciens emit, quas tamen si pro privatis vel profanis deceptus a venditore emerit, habebit actionem ex empto, quod non habere ei liceat, ut consequatur, quod sua interest deceptum eum non esse. Idem iuris est si hominem liberum pro servo emerit.

One who knowingly purchases sacred or religious places, as well as public places such as a forum or basilica, does so without effect. But if someone purchases them, having been misled by the seller into believing that they were capable of private ownership or non-sacred, he will have a buyer's action, because he may not remain in possession. He will then recover the amount of his interest in not being misled. The result is the same if he shall buy a 'slave' who is in fact a free man.

The text adds the *liber homo* at the end and brings it under the same rules, though the rules for the *liber homo* and *res extra commercium* evolved separately, and are assimilated here only because the finer points in the classification of actions were unimportant to Justinian.[42] The buyer of a *res extra commercium* did not in fact receive a proper *actio ex empto* under the classical law, but an *actio in factum*. The separate evolution of these two classes of objects is the subject of two modern studies.[43]

The following is a summary of Daube's views on this evolution. A handful of contrasting views is given in the footnotes.

1. Under the classical law, the sale of a free man is a valid

---

si indica il lato dinamico della suscettibilità o insuscettibilità di rapporti giuridici, con la seconda l'aspetto, per così dire, statico.

[41] The reference to *loca publica* (and elsewhere, *res publicae*) is usually regarded as an addition by Justinian, and interpolated in the various Digest texts where it appears (D.18.1.6 pr. (Pomp. 9 *Sab.*); 18.1.22 (Ulpian 22 *Sab.*); 18.1.62.1 (Modest. 5 *reg.*)). See Stein (note 37), 77–78; MS 145.

[42] For the most part the classical jurists spoke separately of the sale of 'res extra commercium' and 'liber homo', though one text of Paul appears to bring them together. D.18.1.34.1 (Paul 33 *ed.*): *Omnium rerum, quas quis habere vel possidere vel persequi potest, venditio recte fit: quas vero natura vel gentium ius vel mores civitatis commercio exuerunt, earum nulla venditio est.* ('One may properly sell all things that may be held, possessed or sued for. However, one may not sell things which are placed outside commerce by nature, the law of nations or state morals.')

[43] Evans-Jones (note 37); Evans-Jones and MacCormack (note 37).

sale, if the buyer was unaware.[44]
2. To Pomponius/Sabinus,[45] the vendor's knowledge is irrelevant.[46]
3. Under the classical law, the sale of a *locus sacer* or *religiosus* is not a valid sale, as the buyer does not acquire an economic asset. A *locus sacer*, such as a temple, is self-evidently *extra commercium*, though this is not necessarily true of a *locus religiosus*.
4. The classical jurists would give an *actio ex empto* where a free man was purchased, and an *actio in factum* where a *locus sacer* or *religiosus* was purchased.[47]
5. The post-classical lawyers extended the *actio ex empto* to *locus sacer* or *religiosus*, the distinction between that action and the *actio in factum* no longer being meaningful.
6. Justinian (in J.3.23.5) seems to have required fraud on the seller's part before a remedy might be granted to the buyer. This may have been the resolution of a classical dispute, reflected in two texts.[48]

The novelty of Daube's argument emerges from his reconstruction of this central trio of texts:

D.18.1.4 (Pomponius 9 *ad Sabinum*). Et liberi hominis et loci sacri et religiosi, qui haberi non potest, emptio intellegitur, si ab ignorante emitur,

(There may even be a purchase of things that cannot be kept — free persons and sacred and religious land — so long as it is purchased [by? from?] an unknowing person,)

18.1.5 (Paul 5 *ad Sabinum*). quia difficile dinosci potest liber homo a servo.

(because it can be difficult to distinguish a free person from a slave.)

---

[44] Accord: Buckland (note 37), 6; Stein (note 37), 62. Cf. Haymann (note 37), 163 (invalid sale; no *actio*); Biondi (note 37), 11 (valid sale, regardless of the buyer's knowledge); de Zulueta (note 37), 10 (invalid sale); Thomas (note 37), 141 (invalid sale); Evans-Jones (note 37), 475 (valid sale, first recognised when both parties were *ignorans*).
[45] D.18.1.4 (Pomp. 9 *Sab.*), discussed below.
[46] Cf. Stein (note 37), 65 (Sabinus' opinion based on both parties being *ignorans*); Thomas (note 37), 142 (Sabinus expresses no opinion on either party's knowledge).
[47] Accord: Evans-Jones (note 37), 476 (*actio in factum* available against the fraudulent seller of *locus religiosus*). Cf. Stein (note 37), 75 (*actio ex empto* available to buyer of *locus sacer* or *religiosus*).
[48] D.18.1.62.1 (Modest. 5 *reg.*) (appearing to require fraud on the seller's part) and 70 (Licinn. 8 *reg.*) (noting that many jurists require ignorance on the part of both buyer and seller). Accord: Stein (note 37), 66.

18.1.6 pr. (Pomponius *ad Sabinum*). Sed Celsus filius ait hominem liberum scientem te emere non posse nec cuiuscumque rei si scias alienationem [prohibitam *Mom.*] esse: ut sacra et religiosa loca aut quorum commercium non sit, ut publica, quae non in pecunia populi, sed in publico usu habeatur, ut est campus Martius.

(But the younger Celsus says that you cannot knowingly purchase a free person, or indeed anything, if you know that its transfer is forbidden: for example sacred and religious land or land excluded from private commerce, such as public land which is not in public possession but which is kept for public use, like the Field of Mars.)

There is clearly a great deal wrong in the condition of these texts. The erroneous assimilation of the two classes of sale, created by the insertion of *et loci sacri et religiosi* in fragment 4, has caused, in turn, a mismatch between the singular *potest* and its subjects. These two errors, at least, cancel each other out. The *si ab ignorante emitur* remains: it is naturally taken to refer to the unknowing buyer (particularly in view of Justinian's later formulation), but to read it in this way deprives fragment 6 — introduced by *sed* — of all contrast. Not surprisingly, it is usual to remove the contrast by emendation.[49]

Daube's achievement was to preserve both the *si ab ignorante emitur* and the *sed*.[50] From his notes one can reconstruct his emendations as follows.

D.18.1.4 (Pomponius 9 *ad Sabinum*). Et liberi hominis ~~et loci sacri et religiosi, qui haberi non potest~~,[51] emptio intellegitur, si ab ignorante emitur,

---

[49] See, e.g., Stein (note 37), 64 (*si ab ignorante emitur* removed); Thomas (note 37), 140–41 (*si ab ignorante emitur* removed).

[50] Note that Evans-Jones and MacCormack, though they pursue a very different explanation from Daube's, maintain, like Daube, the authenticity of both *si ab ignorante emitur* and *sed*. Evans-Jones (note 37); Evans-Jones and MacCormack (note 37).

[51] The removal of *et loci sacri et religiosi* is not controversial, for the reasons mentioned above. The removal of *qui haberi non potest*, however, is odd, if its authenticity is the basis for the removal of *et loci* etc. Daube suggests *qui haberi non potest* was added by way of generalization, to show that the land could not be 'kept'; it does not, he says, relate to the matter of eviction. The latter point, at least, is sound, for the simple reason that an eviction remedy presumes a valid contract of sale, and 'it is deemed a sale because the buyer might be evicted' would be nonsense. Note, however, that Evans-Jones and MacCormack persuasively argue the reverse proposition, that the desirability of an eviction remedy where the seller was innocent prompted the recognition of a valid sale in the case of the *liber homo*, and that traces of this eviction remedy appear in the words *quod non habere ei liceat* of J.3.23.5: Evans-Jones and MacCormack (note 37), 339, 349; Evans-Jones (note 37), 474–76.

18.1.5 (Paul 5 *ad Sabinum*). quia difficile dinosci potest liber homo a servo.

18.1.6 pr. (Pomponius *ad Sabinum*). Sed Celsus filius ait hominem liberum scientem te emere non posse ~~nec cuiuscumque rei si scias alienationem esse: ut sacra et religiosa loca aut quorum commercium non sit, ut publica, quae non in pecunia populi, sed in publico usu habeatur, ut est campus Martius~~.

The contrast between *si ab ignorante emitur* and *sed* is not, according to Daube, expressed in the text that survives. Daube supplies the contrast by speculating that Celsus, rather than asserting something *different* from Pomponius/Sabinus, was asserting something *more*. Daube would have Celsus say, in a sentence replacing the one which has been removed, that one who knowingly purchases a *locus sacer* or *religiosus* does not have an *actio in factum*. If this is correct, then the contrast could be paraphrased thus: 'Pomponius/Sabinus said that the unknowing buyer of a free man has contracted a sale, *while* Celsus said that, not only does the knowing buyer of a free man fail to contract a sale, but the knowing buyer of a *locus sacer* or *religiosus* will not receive an *actio in factum*.'

Daube's analysis is incomplete; he does not attempt to describe the nature of the classical disputes. However, those who are familiar with his writings on sale will have their suspicions where his analysis is leading. A thesis he returned to again and again concerned a school dispute which he perceived affected sale contracts that were in some respect abortive.

The Sabinians were generally more disposed to assume the existence of a contract of sale than the Proculians, who worked with actions *in factum*.[52]

He introduced the thesis in his 1959 article, 'Certainty of Price'. He argued that a seller who seeks to enforce a *pactum de retrovendendo* (a term allowing a seller to repurchase on a certain event) would proceed *ex empto* according to the Sabinians, *in factum* according to the Proculians.[53] He suggested the same would be true for the enforcement of a term

---

[52] D. Daube, 'Condition Prevented from Materializing', *Tijdschrift voor Rechtsgeschiedenis*, 28 (1960), 283.

[53] See C.4.54.2 (AD 222); D.19.5.12 (Proc. 11 *epist.*); Daube, 'Certainty of Price' (note 9), 32.

setting a price partly by reference to a further sale by the buyer.[54] Then:

> The conflict between the schools was of a rather fundamental nature, the Sabinians sponsoring and the Proculians declining the main contractual action in many other cases — cases of an incipient contract, or of a contract which fails, or of the remoter effects of a contract.[55]

Daube later detected the same school dispute where a buyer had deliberately frustrated a conditional sale[56] and where a seller had deliberately frustrated the sale of future fruits or offspring.[57]

The texts above on the sale of the *liber homo* and *res extra commercium* are open to the same interpretation. Fragments 4 and 6 contrast two views of an abortive sale, without making the nature of the contrast clear. Daube had found some degree of contrast by supposing that the younger Celsus (a Proculian) considered the application of actions *in factum* where *res extra commercium* are purchased. Daube says nothing about school disputes. But we can easily suppose that, in time, he would have suggested that some state of affairs — perhaps the inadequacy of the available remedies — prompted the schools to put forward their favoured remedies: the Sabinians an action on the sale, the Proculians an action *in factum*. Daube may even have taken the view that a Proculian would give *in factum* in the case of the *liber homo*, and that this is the controversy the compilers have hidden from view in the three texts (and particularly the mangled D.18.1.6 pr.).[58] We have some unlikely evidence that Daube was leaning in this direction from a 1983 piece written by Yoav Ben-Dror.[59] Daube appears to have helped with the piece,

---

[54] Daube, 'Certainty of Price' (note 9), 31–32
[55] Id., 32.
[56] Daube, 'Condition Prevented from Materializing' (note 52), 283–84 (on D.18.1.50 (Ulpian 11 *ed.*)).
[57] Id., 287 (on D.18.1.8 pr. (Pomp. 9 *Sab.*)).
[58] A convenient hypothesis for explaining D.18.1.70 (Licinn. 8 *reg.*): *Liberi hominis emptionem contrahi posse plerique existimaverunt, si modo inter ignorantes id fiat*. Were the Proculians the dissenters, with their grudging actions *in factum*?
[59] Y. Ben-Dror, 'The Perennial Ambiguity of *Culpa in Contrahendo*', *Journal of Legal History*, 27:2 (1983), 142–98.

and is acknowledged.⁶⁰ Writing on D.18.1.6 pr., Ben-Dror says:⁶¹

> It seems that the original text draws a line between two categories: *liber homo* on the one hand and *locus sacer* and *locus religiosus* on the other. Pomponius stated that, according to the younger Celsus, the sale of a free man is invalid if the buyer knows that he is a free man. Pomponius went on to say that, similarly, there is no *actio in factum* for *locus sacer* or *locus religiosus* if the buyer knows the real nature of his purchase.

A reader will examine the text in vain for mention of an *actio in factum*: Ben-Dror has stated Daube's hypothesis perfectly. Further along, Ben-Dror describes the broad school dispute on sale actions and actions *in factum* put forward by Daube. Then, in a footnote Ben-Dror writes: 'This explains Dig. Just. 18.1.4, 5, & 6.'⁶² Ben-Dror, in short, appears to be stating Daube's otherwise unrecorded opinion.

Teaching to interpret

Readers of Daube's published works know the kind of scholar he was. He did not aspire to be a system builder; to set out rules precisely and elegantly; to construct grand theories of societal evolution; to treat laws as social facts. His method, as Alan Rodger once described it in a public lecture, was to consider a text and to ask, as an initial matter, why the text is expressed as it is.⁶³ In a companion piece to that lecture I considered Daube's method in detail, finding it to be deeply anti-positivist and at the same time meticulously scientific: if one's goal is to explain texts 'causally', as Daube did, then every 'cause' one discovers and isolates is a new weapon in the reader's arsenal, permitting the reader to discover more precise explanations for an ever-widening number of texts.⁶⁴

---

⁶⁰ Id., 142.
⁶¹ Id., 164–65.
⁶² Id., 167 n.157.
⁶³ A. Rodger, 'Law for All Times: The Work and Contribution of David Daube', in E. Metzger, ed., *Law for All Times. Essays in Memory of David Daube* [*Roman Legal Tradition*, 2] (Lawrence, KS 2004), 11–14.
⁶⁴ E. Metzger, 'Quare? Argument in David Daube, After Karl Popper', in E. Metzger, ed., *Law for All Times. Essays in Memory of David Daube* [*Roman Legal Tradition*, 2] (Lawrence, KS 2004), 27–58.

Naturally this is a method of interpretation which Daube followed equally in his teaching. Gordon:[65]

What helped to enliven his lectures was his explanations of why the law was as he said it was and how it was likely to have come into being. It was not simply an exposition of the rules but an exposition of the reason for them.

To describe how a rule came into being is partly a historical exercise, but in Daube's hands also an exercise in imagination. The rule announced in a text can be the product of generalization, abbreviation, misunderstanding, shortness of time, transmission error, hesitation, enthusiasm, vanity, or pettiness. A jurist may change his mind, express himself badly, inflate a minor point, diminish an inconvenient fact, or fabricate a controversy.

We know that any of these factors and limitless others can leave its mark on a text and help us to understand it. But the lesson must be learned. A student, left to himself, will not attempt to understand a text in this way, but instead perversely turn the text into something he can understand. The texts on the *liber homo* and *res extra commercium* illustrate the point. If a teacher asks a student to describe the law, the student will probably answer with a single statement: 'an innocent buyer of a *liber homo* or *res extra commercium* has contracted a valid sale'. But simplicity comes at a cost: the student has actively ignored factors that brought the texts to their present condition, not to mention the little tics and flashes by which the jurists have given away their meaning unconsciously. Daube knew that the more acute reader will be able to describe the law more accurately than the less acute, and he taught his students accordingly.

Daube, in other words, was not teaching his students to be advocates, who embark on interpretation in the expectation that a single statement of the law is waiting at the finish. Advocates, disagreements notwithstanding, compete to reach the same goal. It is therefore no wonder, having set themselves a fixed distance to travel, that they avoid imagining other paths that would lengthen the journey, or that they

---

[65] Gordon (note 1), 95 (speaking of Daube's Roman law lectures at ordinary level).

shorten the journey by adhering to fixed rules of interpretation. Daube encouraged his students to take the longer journey.

> A very plausible emendation. I don't believe in it.[66]

---

[66] MS 133 (on D.18.1.20 (Pomp. 9 *Sab.*)).

Appendix

David Daube — Lectures on Sale D. 18.1. 1–24

Lecture No. 3 (excerpt: MS 21–28)

We come now to the controversial fragment 4. This comes from Pomponius's section on the contract of sale, so again, as regards the original context, it is in order. As it stands, the text says that the sale of a free man or of a locus sacer or religiosus that cannot be held — privately held, I suppose — is possible so long as the buyer is ignorant of the quality of the object.

First of all let me note that we have not to do here with eviction. The question is not what the buyer of such objects may do if he is evicted, but whether the sale is valid, i.e., whether it is enforceable when the buyer discovers the quality of the object, enforceable in the sense that he can ask for his interest — for damages.

As the text stands it says that the contract is enforceable: there is a sale. Haymann regards the decision as entirely due to Justinian, and therefore he rewrites the text. According to him, it originally ran 'nec liberi hominis, nec loci sacri, nec religiosi, emptio intellegitur'. So you have the opposite decision; no sale of any of those things is recognised. Others, less radical, cross out the three words 'sacri et religiosi' because they say that it is enough to speak of a piece of land which cannot be held — 'qui haberi non potest'. However, it is very dangerous to cross out a few words because they are included in a more general expression. If one does start crossing out, and you will see that I shall do so quite soon, one should cross out the general definition and leave the more particular cases in. If we did resort to crossing out in this connection, it would be more probable that 'qui haberi non potest' should be considered as added — the wider expression — and that the narrow references to locus sacer and locus religiosus would be original.

Many authorities reject the very last clause, which says that this sale is valid 'if the buyer does not know about the quality'. The reason is that this reservation recurs in fragment 6, which is also from Pomponius, and therefore they say it is here superfluous: it is a generalization of a particular decision recorded in fragment 6. It does not matter much, because it does not alter the state of the law. Even the authorities who reject these final few words admit that if the buyer knows of the quality, then the sale is not enforceable.

Now for the crossing out to which I shall subscribe. Some scholars cross out the whole passage from 'et loci sacri' up to 'potest'. I shall tell you why I subscribe to this. All these things are rather conjectural, but it is better to take a view rather than leave everything undecided. I think that Pomponius admitted an enforceable sale in the case of a free man if the buyer did not know that he was free. But in the case of locus sacer and locus religiosus, I think in classical law there were other remedies. The remedy might be an actio doli, e.g. if the vendor knew. The remedy might be condictio, whether the vendor knew or not. Condictio if you had paid something. And the remedy might even be an actio in factum, which would give you much the same as an actio ex empto. My reason for assuming this will come later. We shall find references to an actio in factum in such cases.

Naturally, for the Byzantines and compilers, the difference between an actio in factum and an actio ex empto meant very little. While Pomponius distinguished between a free man and locus sacer or religiosus, giving actio empti in the former case and actio in factum in the latter, the compilers put all the cases together, because these subtleties of the formulary system did not count for them.

A question we have to ask is: Why was there a difference between these cases in classical law? Why should there be an actio ex empto in the case of a free man and an actio in factum in the case of locus sacer or religiosus? Well, one reason which seems to have been mentioned by the classical lawyers will come in fragment 5: it is very difficult to distinguish a free man from a slave by the look of him, and the legal situation may be in doubt. A man may think himself he is a slave and may be free; remember the bona fide serviens. That will come in fragment 5, and I would point out that in fragment 5, as we shall see, mention is made only of the free man but not of locus sacer and locus religiosus. Paul in fragment 5 refers only to the liber homo.

But there may have been a further reason for the distinction. After all, it may be difficult to see from a piece of land whether a man was buried there or not; so locus religiosus may be difficult to distinguish from ordinary land — though, to be sure there would be normally be a tombstone. At any rate, a reason for the distinction between free man and locus sacer or religiosus which has been suggested, and which seems to be quite plausible, is this. If I acquire a free man in the belief that he is a slave, I do really acquire an economic asset, since, although he is free, you will remember that whatever I acquire through him — ex operis or ex re — vests in me, not in him. But when I acquire a locus sacer or religiosus, I do not acquire a true economic asset. That seems to be a relevant difference.

In classical law, then, in the case of a free man, if the buyer did not know, there seems to have been an action on the contract, in the case of locus sacer or religiosus an action in factum. The post-classical lawyers extended the validity of the sale and gave actio empti also where it was a question of a piece of land. They emphasised that extension by saying that the action should lie for any piece of land 'qui haberi non potest', which was extra commercium. We find the extension in Justinian's Institutes 3.23.5, where land and free men are equated.

Now as regards knowledge. From the text which is before us it appears that the knowledge or otherwise of the vendor is irrelevant. However, in Justinian 3.23.5 it looks as if the vendor must know, must be dolose, if he is to be answerable, because there is something about deceptus in the text. It is not absolutely certain, but it very much looks as if fraud — knowledge on the part of the vendor — were required. This would accord with Byzantine moralizing tendencies.

In our title there are two interesting texts to which we shall come, namely fragment 62.1, from Modestinus, where again it looks — because the word decipere is used — as if fraud were required if you want to get full damages. I say 'it looks'; I am not certain, because I suppose it could be argued that 'ne deciperetur' is used in an objective sense: the buyer has been — not 'deceived' but — 'disappointed', he has been let down whether or not the lender knew. Or it may be argued that Modestinus uses traditional language coming from ancient promises by the vendor not to cheat, but that he would not confine the action to fraud. However, 'decipere' does suggest fraud. On the other hand, in fragment 70, from Licinnius Rufinus, it is made quite clear that by most authorities fraud is not required: 'si modo inter ignorantes id fiat'. So there seems to have been a problem here, perhaps a dispute, and Justinian appears to require fraud, although I am not absolutely certain.

Another problem is again connected with fragment 70. Fragment 70 at first sight seems to show that even in the case of a free man there were lasting doubts whether a sale was enforceable: 'plerique existimaverunt', 'most authorities have held'. But possibly the doubts expressed here are not about enforceability of such a sale in general, but only about its enforceability if the vendor was innocent, did not know that the man was free. Licinnius Rufinus may intend to say that 'most authorities held' that full damages were due even if the vendor did not know that the man was free, 'si modo inter ignorantes id fiat'.

And now one more remark, and this is of a kind every Roman lawyer likes to make, because every Roman lawyer likes to be able to show that a colleague and friend of his is wrong. That is a natural quality of Roman lawyers, and de Zulueta in his book on sale p. 10 note 7 commits a blunder, and, of course, it is wonderful! It is a very small mistake (and I have told him).[67] He says that in principle the sale of a liber homo was void. In principle it was void but gradually it was allowed. In note 7, the first text he adduces to support this principle is from Justinian's Institutes 3.19.2. Well, this text should not be quoted in this connection. His other text is all right, but this text is not because it speaks about stipulatio — not about sale. Now we must not transfer the principles of

---

[67] [De Zulueta did not, however, amend the note for the 1957 edition.]

stipulatio to sale. Why not? In stipulatio I maintain that the other party should dare the object, 'Stichum dare oportere', he is under a civil law obligation to transfer the object. Well, once I have found out this is a free man, then in principle I cannot claim such a thing — I cannot claim that you should at civil law convey a free man to me. In sale I claim something quite different — 'quidquid dare facere oportet ex fide bona', whatever may be due to me on the ground of good faith. I may claim damages on the ground of good faith even when it turns out that this man is free. So the text which says that once you have discovered that this man is free you cannot in principle bring the action under the stipulatio is no proof that you can't bring an action under sale in classical law, because the formula is quite different.

Well, now, we come to fragment 5, which is from Paul, and it is from Paul where he discusses the contract of sale, so it is all right so far as the original context goes. It just says that it is difficult to distinguish a free man from a slave.

I have pointed out that this fragment applies to free men — not to land. Let us ask how far the reason would, in fact, apply to land. It would hardly apply to locus sacer because you would usually be able to distinguish a temple from a private dwelling-house, although nowadays some of the private dwelling houses do look like non-conformist chapels. We have one at the Grammar School end of Osborne Place. But often it would also be easy to see that land is locus religiosus, because usually there would be a tombstone.

Regarding locus publicus, the term 'locus publicus' may mean two things; it may mean a piece of land which happens for the moment to belong to the state but which the state at any moment might sell, and it might mean things like public baths or the Campus Martius — land permanently and intrinsically dedicated to public use. In the latter case again it must often be quite easy to see that the thing is public — and if it is not public in the sense of permanently devoted to public use, no special rules apply. It must be easy to distinguish a forum or a theatre. But occasionally — and we shall see that these cases had a certain importance, being mentioned, e.g., in clauses of the contract — you would not be able to say at once whether a piece of land was public or not. For instance, you might not be sure whether a certain corner of a road belongs to the road or not; it might belong to the adjoining private estate.

We will now go on to fragment 6, and this also comes from Pomponius on sale. As the text stands — I shall not read words which modern editors (such as Mommsen) have inserted — it tells a confused story.

The younger Celsus holds that the sale of a free man is not valid if the buyer knows that he is free. Nor is the transfer of anything valid if you know. Then we are given the examples of locus sacer and locus religiosus or things — yes, it says 'or' things — which are extra commercium, such as public places, which do not just happen to belong to the populus but which are permanently in public use, such as the Campus Martius.

Clearly, this fragment has been interfered with. It is rather confused. First let us see what Haymann makes of it. He crosses out 'sed' because, according to him, sale of a free man is always void in classical law whether the buyer knows or not. So he crosses out 'sed'. He cannot tolerate a contrast with the preceding fragments as reconstructed by him. He also crosses out 'scientem', because the sale is always void. And then he crosses out everything from 'cuiuscumque' up to the word 'sacra', so that he obtains 'Celsus ait hominum [sic] liberum te emere non posse, nec sacra aut religiosa loca', i.e. 'you can't buy a free man, locus sacer and locus religiosus also cannot be bought'. Such is his theory, but it goes too far for me. Other learned authorities cross out everything from 'nec cuiuscumque' right to the end of the text, because from 'nec cuiuscumque' you must admit that the text as it stands is unsatisfactory.

I think the text has suffered both abbreviation and addition. From 'nec cuiuscumque it makes no sense and the Latin is bad. No valid sale of a free man if you know — nor a transfer or anything if you know, or perhaps, nor a sale of anything if you know that it is alienation; it is ridiculous. It is simply absurd. Mommsen, following inferior manuscripts, inserted the word 'prohibitam', but that is Mommsen, not the text. Moreover, even with Mommsen's insertion the genitive 'cuiuscumque rei' would be in the air. You cannot knowingly buy a free man or 'of anything' if you know that transfer is prohibited: very bad Latin. Then there comes a difficulty also in the next part, because the text speaks of loca sacra and religiosa 'or' things which are not in commercio. Surely, loca sacra and religiosa are not in commercio. So why mention these and continue 'or things extra commercium'? Here we have a generalization tacked on to specific cases in a manner similar to that which we found in fragment 4 — 'qui haberi non potest'.

I will tell you what I think Pomponius said. He said that, according to Celsus, the sale of a free man is not valid if you, the buyer, know he is free. Then, I think, he went on to say that, similarly, there is no actio in factum for locus sacer or locus religiosus if you know about the quality. In fact this division he makes between a free man and a locus sacer or religiosus — and he obviously did discuss them one after the other instead of together — supports the thesis that there was only an actio in factum in the case of locus sacer or religiosus. Pomponius obviously had two quite different sentences. He did not say: You cannot knowingly buy a free man, a locus sacer or a locus religiosus. He first dealt with the free man, refusing action on the contract, and then with locus sacer or religiosus, refusing actio in factum.

The public land may possibly have been added later. Now why? This creates a difficulty. In fragment 22 of our title there is also a strong indication that the public land is added, because it does not appear in the first part, in the clause of the contract, but only in the second part, after 'ceterum si'. On the other hand, in fragment 72.1 I see no reason to regard the public land as added. Here it seems to be alright. Well, then, supposing the public land in fragment 6 is added, why did Pomponius not speak about it? Let me insert that I am not sure that it is a later addition. Possibly he did speak about it, and the fact that he does so in a separate clause may be explicable by his intention of making the distinction between land which was only for the moment belonging to the state but could be trafficked in and land permanently and essentially public. But it is also possible that the whole thing about public land is added. Well, if so, we may conclude that this case was really less important than the other cases, because usually — although not always — public land could easily be distinguished from other land. Usually you had no difficulty in noticing a theatrum or forum. However, where such land was not distinguishable — say, the end of a public road — I suppose that in principle the same rules would have applied to public land as applied to locus sacer or locus religiosus.

VIII

David Daube: A Personal Reminiscence

Alan Watson[*]

Professor Watson writes about his time, both personally and professionally, as Daube's doctoral student, then colleague.

I am delighted to be again in Aberdeen, a city I have long loved — as did David. He often told me now happy he had been in the city and university. He often also told me that if the Germans had invaded Britain in World War II, in Aberdeen he would have been protected, in Oxford he would have been betrayed. He often gave me relevant cryptic messages. For instance, when I accepted an invitation to give some lectures in the DDR, he cautioned me to say nothing in favour of the regime: that when he was in the Soviet Union and wanted to know how things were, he would visit a Jewish barber in Samarkand.

* * *

David Daube provided me with the greatest possible support for a young scholar. I shall devote this paper first of all to my relationship with him when I was writing my doctoral thesis, 'The Contract of Mandate in Roman Law',[1] under his supervision (1957–1959).

But at the outset let me say what he did not do for me.

---

[*] Distinguished Research Professor and Ernest P. Rogers Chair of Law, University of Georgia School of Law.
[1] Bodleian Library, Oxford University, MS. D.Phil. c.369.

Alan Watson, 'David Daube: A Personal Reminiscence', in E. Metzger, ed., *David Daube: A Centenary Celebration* (Glasgow: Traditio Iuris Romani, 2010), 127–37. Copyright © 2010 by Alan Watson (content) and Ernest Metzger (typographical arrangement). All rights reserved.
ROMANLEGALTRADITION.ORG

First, he never gave me any help with finding the primary sources. He clearly felt that that was a job for a doctoral candidate to do for himself. I agree totally with Daube. If a doctoral candidate cannot find the requisite material he should find a more suitable job. I freely admit, though, that I was much helped for finding the sources by a then recent book by a great scholar, Vincenzo Arangio-Ruiz, on the subject: *Il mandato in diritto romano*.[2] Of course, the existence of that book presented me with a different challenge. My thesis would only be worthwhile if it said something very different. Arangio-Ruiz was a wonderful older man who was very friendly towards me and to others. When I gave my first international paper which disagreed with him on a different subject, he hugged me warmly and said to the audience that I was his nemesis, put on earth to keep him straight. When in my thesis I referred to him as a 'great Italian scholar' David rebuked me: I should not refer to someone by his ethnic or national origin.

Secondly, David never said a word to me about the existing tools of the trade that were intended to help even the experienced scholar find his way into the sources. For Roman law such sources are bountiful. For instance, there is the multi-volume *Vocabularium Iurisprudentiae Romanae* that lists the place of occurrences in Justinian's Digest of every word in all its forms. There is a similar *Vocabularium* for Justinian's Institutes and another for Gaius' Institutes. Again, the journal *IURA* publishes in its annual volume a short account of every relevant legal article published in the preceding year listing all the legal terms referred to in Latin or Greek.

Thirdly, he did not point me to articles or books that I should read or should have read with the sole exception of W. W. Buckland (who had done so much for him when he came to Britain) and himself (which was an indication of his proper self-esteem).

But what he did for me was much more important. He would demand that I write a chapter for him, about one per month. As soon as I delivered it he would fix a date, always

---

[2] Naples 1949.

within two weeks, for me to come and lunch with him in All Souls. He was always affable but, lunch over, we would go to his rooms where we went over the chapter sentence by sentence. His examination was rigorous and awe-inspiring, and I was always terrified. His most frightening criticism was 'Oho!' Then I knew I had made a superlative blunder. We broke for tea for half-an-hour then back to the same ordeal until seven when I had to return to Wadham for dinner. He was incredibly learned, and continually made me think again. But never, except once when my chapter was very unsatisfactory, did he ever ask to see my revisions or ask to read a chapter again. (Indeed, for some time I did not even understand what the issue for that chapter was. And David did not enlighten me.) I was left to stand on my own feet after he had given his great wisdom. At the end of each session he would leave me with words of encouragement as well as fixing a date when I would hand in my next chapter.

But this was only the beginning of the help he gave me. He made me into a member of his family, not in the sense of knowing the details of his relationship with his wife (stormy) and his sons (often not easy), but I could drop in at his home rather freely, often had Sabbath lunch with the family, he introduced me to a great number of his friends, I imbibed — almost by osmosis — much of German Jewish behaviour, and a sense of pre-war sophisticated German academic civil and polite behaviour. It should be remembered that, although only a small percentage of German Jewish intellectuals survived the Nazis, those that I met through David were those who had come to Britain and by 1957 had reached the top tier of intellectuals there. Many others who had come to Britain and were still alive had not made it to near the top of intellectual life. (Theirs was a sad case, not living up to their potential.[3]) But I did not meet them. Nor did I much meet

---

[3] Two names spring to mind: Fritz Schulz who died before I came to Oxford but had written books, two of which I regard as outstanding: *Principles of Roman Law* and *Roman Legal Science*. But he never held a decent academic post. I learned something about him from his widow. The other is Fritz Pringsheim whom I did meet and who also had written distinguished works on ancient law. He was very bitter, and could not forget his early days of success in Germany. I did not enjoy his company. I should write more, but this is not the place.

through David those of Russian origins. But I did meet the Italians, notably Arnaldo Momigliano and Lorenzo Minio-Paluello, both of whom became good friends.

Not long after I arrived in Oxford, David and his wife Herta gave a small party and I was invited. There I was talking with an elderly woman who asked if I would come and have tea with her one day. I agreed and had a splendid time. There were four attractive young women there, and they all made much of me. When I left I was full of happiness. I had made a transition from a poor unattractive student to an attractive Oxford don. I never heard from the elderly lady again. I had mentioned I was engaged to be married. I eventually realized that for a brief time I had entered the old central European tradition of match-making. Although he did not say so, David was delighted.

I completed my D. Phil. with David within two years, but the woman I hired to type it was pregnant and often sick, and one of my examiners was Patrick Duff, Regius Professor of Civil Law in Cambridge. He was the first lazy and worthless Oxbridge don that I met. It took six months for my oral exam to take place. Duff explained that he was so busy it was not easy for him to get from his college, Trinity, to the Squire Law Library. The buildings are about 150 yards apart. As a result I graduated in 1960 instead of, as I had hoped, 1959. I mention Duff because of my disappointment in him. Not all successful dons were like David.

To my delight, my book, *Contract of Mandate in Roman Law*,[4] was, thanks to David, accepted for publication by the Clarendon Press. I made the customary acknowledgments and thanked Duff for his help especially with regard to my English style. His sole contribution had been to make a few changes to my commas. A French reviewer noted as a result that I, as a non-Englishmen, was touchingly aware of my inadequate knowledge of the language.

I dedicated the book as I think was proper, to David Daube and Tony Thomas who had taught me at Glasgow. Thomas wrote: 'You need not have bothered.' I thought he was being

---

[4] Oxford 1961.

modest. Alas, I was deceived.[5]

A marked characteristic of David was his generosity both of money and of spirit. For instance, whenever I visited Berkeley he would insist that I stay — at his cost — at the Women's Faculty Club: 'It is much more interesting than the Men's Club.' One morning at breakfast we were joined by a visiting physicist who insisted that women were much more aggressive than men. David disputed the claim but the scientist was not persuaded. Hours later when David and I were walking on the beach at Sausalito he said 'Look here, Alan, if the spermatozoon was not more aggressive it would never fertilize the egg.' He had a wicked sense of fun. Once, when I was his guest for lunch in All Souls, the guest of another fellow was the Provost of Eton. It was suggested that we all sit together. David introduced me: 'This is Alan Watson. He speaks only *classical* Greek at lunch.'

To jump ahead. Many years later there was a conference in Bonn on the impact of German refugee scholars on British and American law. I was asked to talk about David. He was too frail to attend so I went to Berkeley to see him. He lamented that this was the first year he had been too ill to spend the summer in Germany, a country and land that he adored. I remarked that he was the last-surviving legal scholar trained in the pre-Nazi German fashion. He remarked sadly, 'No. You are.'

I never saw him again. Years later at a meeting in Dublin I met a professor from the Hebrew University who told me that shortly before his death she went to visit him and that he had a book of mine in each hand.

Though my intention in this paper was primarily to set out the beginning of my relationship with David it is fitting to close with a letter of his from Berkeley dated 17 October 1995.

---

[5] I wrote my final examination paper for Thomas, 'Arra in the law of Justinian', the subject on which Thomas had published his own first Roman law article. He gave me the highest possible grade but refused to discuss the paper with me. When I began to lecture on the Roman law of sale at Oxford, I dug out my paper, revised it and showed it to David who, without my knowledge, sent it to Fernand de Visscher who published it in *RIDA*. Thereafter some scholars became much less friendly. I was puzzled but later was told that Tony bad-mouthed me. Alas! Thomas passed on his hostility to others whom I will not name.

The letter illustrates his abiding care for me and the intensity of his scholarly help. It was sent in response to my first book on law in the Gospels, *Jesus and the Jews: the Pharisaic Tradition in John.*[6]

My dear Alan,

How can I thank you? It is hardly credible — but your work did keep me fascinated from beginning to end when I can hardly read a third of a page of any other. Perhaps the effect of happy surprise? I would never have thought that one with your background, no matter how enormously your perspective extended over the years, would become a top-class expert on the New Testament. In fact, I acknowledge you as definitely my superior by now in that field. A wonderful gift in the midst of growing deprivation.

Your study testifies to your knowledge, your reasoning power, your historical imagination, all fired and tamed by enormous comprehensive direction. I know of no work that surpasses yours — and am surprised to hear you are going to get a Festschrift: I thought it would take another fifty years for your achievement to be appreciated, it is so outstanding. One feature that distinguishes your recent products is that you waste little time justifying your route and refuting less effective approaches. You fully succeed: one is so quickly taken in by your superior guidance that one forgets about useless preconceptions.

Your case for S is absolutely convincing and of enormous importance in many respects.

A few minor items. Ch. 1 p. 8 towards end. I still think that one meaning on top of another in John is more likely than a single one: what I indicate in Catholic Commission on Intellectual and Cultural Affairs Annual 1986, pp. 3-5.[7] Remember Philo!

Ch. 3 p. 8. John 2.10 rather speaks against the wine being frowned on. P. 10 toward the end. I see no ruining

---

[6] Athens, GA, 1995.
[7] [D. Daube, 'Some Reflections on the Historicity of the New Testament' (1986), reprinted in C. Carmichael, ed., *New Testament Judaism* [Collected Works of David Daube, 2] (Berkeley 2000), 35–42.]

of the celebration. P. 12/13. Rather speculative. But I agree that there must be an as yet hidden element. The bridegroom seems to be the beneficiary and is congratulated: meaning?

Ch. 4 p. 1. 'Jews and Samaritans' is not quite exact: the former do not co-use with the latter. Similarly misleading 'Samaritans and Jews' in the last two lines. The relation was perhaps fluid for a long time, but in this story it is the Jews who stand off. P.21 4 from bottom: are you not refusing to fall in with the story?

Ch. 5 p. 11. 3 from bottom. When, by the end of the next century, you will be among the half dozen NT experts still consulted, the nature of the pot you are referring to will be the subject of lively controversy. Pp. 2–4. Is the reaction to Nicodemus hostile? Is it not that more faith is now required than in Matthew's time and milieu — what I am after in my Judas?[8] P. 6. Jesus brutal? Everything is stricter than in Matthew.

Ch. 6 p. 6 towards end. Is it necessarily inconsistent? Why could it not indicate unhurried action to be properly appreciated by all? P. 7 towards end. Very interesting argument.

Ch. 7 p. 2. Are you de-symbolizing John overmuch? P. 3 bottom. Seductively clear. So is p. 4 middle. I always assumed the realistic background that you postulate at the bottom of the page. P. 5 first 12 lines. I am not yet quite convinced. As for Lazarus, the general effect of the miracle *and*, at that time, the wonder for the family were enhanced by the unhurried certainty and performance. P. 8 1. 4ff. A strong argumentation.

Ch. 8 p. 6. A complicated story. P. 8. Your attitude may be too modern. To display his eminence by trustfully delaying a day or two would not in the case of an adult patient be seen as stone-hearted? There are parallels. After all, you might ask why he waits till he gets approached? One consideration surely is achievement of public effectiveness.

---

[8] [D. Daube, 'Judas' (1995), reprinted in C. Carmichael, ed., *New Testament Judaism* [Collected Works of David Daube, 2] (Berkeley 2000), 783–99.]

Ch. 9 p. 2 middle. I still tend to stick to CCICA 1986.[9] John is not 'inaccurate'. P. 7. Your explanation may be too narrow. The action is apocalyptic. Hence he attacks the animals as well as the vendors, he even overthrows the tables. P. 10. Nowadays it is hard to imagine the risk I ran by basing on Eisler. End of page: yes, and none the less I have a feeling that there is still a riddle here. P. 12 l[ine] 1f. Is there a clear difference between Luke and John? L[ine] 5ff. This is very impressive. P. 13. Very impressive though I am not sure I follow fully — I am very ill and hampered in sorting things out. P. 14f. Very interesting and ingenious.

Ch. 10 p. 6. Very ingenious, maybe too exact and exacting? But I am convinced.

Ch. 11 p. 2. Enormously complicated. Anyhow, does 5.16 represent Jesus as 'healing by forcing another to work'? I doubt it. On the other hand, 5.17 is very reminiscent of Philo Legum Allegoria 1.3 (quoted by Strack-Billerbeck). Pp. 3f. Bold, but I accept it.

Ch. 12 p. 7. I have to work out how this bears on New Testament and Rabbinic Judaism pp. 308f.[10]

Ch. 13 p. 2 last line. Do you mean 4.26?

Ch. 14 p. 3 middle. Even with the qualification 'of a bitter kind', 'humour' is a daring term. Do let it stand by all means. It makes one think.

Ch. 15 p. 4. John 3.3 – 3.31 difficult. P. 7. Is the enormous violence in the Johannine cleansing meant literally at any stage? I do not think so. See above. P. 9. As for Matthew 15, he does not 'repent'. To get the right approach here, I think one has to consider the gulf between old Jewish atmosphere and the Hellenistic (in Luke, above all). Second half of p. 9. I tend to accept your results — they are very important. P. 10 last line. Yes, in John above all.

Ch. 17 p. 2. As you translate fraudulosa by 'fraudulent' on page 1, it is perhaps unwise to translate *dolo malo* by 'fraudulently' here. I have every understanding for your

---

[9] [Above, note 7.]
[10] [D. Daube, *The New Testament and Rabbinic Judaism* (London 1956).]

dismissing Roman Law exactitude at the end of a profound disquisition about John. Still .... P. 5. I dismissed interpolation from the first moment. By now I have re-read your excellent article in Studies.[11] One could perhaps add a few points: they would just be further confirmation.

Being full of admiration for your outstanding achievement in Law and History — I shall not even try to find words for the miracle of Sarah. My gratitude to you and Camilla for a photo which I shall keep henceforth.

The letter indicates David's abiding love of scholarship, his acumen, his generosity of spirit, and his continuing interest in his students (even of many years before). It can be no surprise that a photo of him sits on my desk. Nor is it surprising that my son, David, is named after him.

Afterword

I started my university career in 1957 as lecturer in law at Wadham College, Oxford, moving to Oriel in 1959 as Benn Law Fellow. During this time I was given deferment from national service. When my D. Phil. thesis was accepted, I received my call-up papers and was horrified. I had thought for two years about conscription and had become fairly *au fait* with the issue. At once I rushed to David in All Souls, explained my situation to him: high school teachers and technical college lecturers were exempt, but not university lecturers. I expected some sympathy for my plight, but received none. David then danced me to the gate of All Souls to the song Figaro sang to Cherubino when he was sent to military duty. Then he said: 'It is inconceivable that you will be required for military service. You would ruin the British Army!'

That same afternoon he took a train to London to meet with Lord Hailsham, then Chancellor of the Exchequer and a Quondam — that is, a former Fellow of All Souls — and explained the situation. I knew none of this until I received a letter from the Vice-Chancellor of Oxford: 'You will be glad to know you will not be required for military service.' Sir Mau-

---

[11] [A. Watson, 'The Definition of *furtum* and the Trichotomy' (1960), reprinted in *Studies in Roman Private Law* (London 1991), 269–82.]

rice Bowra, Warden of Wadham (where I began my career), said to me: 'My boy, theses will be written on this stage of your career!'

I have written this afterword for all that it reveals about David. 1. His devotion to his students. He put himself to great trouble on my account. 2. His great charm which he could use quite deliberately. 3. His great political sense that he could exploit with influential people, though he also used his skills with the poor and needy. 4. His wonderful gift of friendship. 5. His sense of fun.

David, I love you and miss you every day.

Postscript 1.

Shortly after my appointment at Wadham, David said to me that there were three sides to the academic life, teaching, scholarship and administration, and that it was not possible to do all three well, and asked my intentions. I replied, 'Scholarship and teaching.' David was an outstanding expert in all three.

Postscript 2.

In 1957 I bought my first antiquarian law book: Dionysius Gothofredus, *Corpus Juris Civilis Romani* (Frankfurt and Leipzig, 1705). The price was three guineas and my salary then was six hundred pounds *per annum*. I told David about it, and, was astonished by his response. He looked at me, rather sadly, and said: 'You should have bought a girl a pretty frock.' Only after I had finished writing this reminiscence did it occur to me that he was hinting I should lighten up.

Postscript 3.

David was very angry with me once. I had written a book, *Legal Transplants: an Approach to Comparative Law*.[12] I sent a draft to David who was then at Berkeley and, without consulting me, he sent it to William McClung who was in charge of the University of California Press. Bill wrote me an enthusiastic letter, but subsequently wrote that he could not

---

[12] Edinburgh 1974.

publish because he had received a very negative report. He returned my typescript which was covered with very unpleasant comments, from Arthur Schiller (of Columbia).

I was upset, not least because I had no secretary and would have to retype the manuscript — with one finger. I had also sent a copy to a colleague who replied that I should hide the manuscript because it would spoil my reputation. I set the book aside for four years. Much later that colleague told me he was a very jealous individual, and was jealous of my manuscript. David did not hide his anger that for the first time I had rejected his judgment.

Postscript 4.

When I accepted the Chair of Civil Law at Edinburgh, David told me that I would meet extreme hostility from Tom Smith, that I could handle it, but if not I should report to him. I did receive such opposition to such an extent that the Principal of the university compelled Smith to write me a letter of apology. I did not report to David.

Postscript 5.

Again, I was told that David had twice written to Professor John Smith, then in charge of the Law Section of the British Academy, recommending that I be elected a Fellow. Another indication of his continuing concern for his pupils.

Whether David ever received a reply, I do not know.

Postscript 6.

Once I received a letter from Laurent Mayali (who was in charge of the Robbins Collection at Berkeley) that he was soliciting donations: David was becoming frail and needed a wheel-chair. I immediately sent him a cheque to cover the cost of an electric wheel-chair. Mayali wrote that David did not use it. But years later David wrote: 'How prescient of you to know that one day I would need a wheelchair.'

IX

David Daube

Jonathan M. Daube[*]

These notes are dedicated to Shoshana Yaron, who died in Israel while they were being prepared, and to Kathleen Vanden Heuvel, who is alive and well in California.

They loved David Daube for who he was.

David Daube was born in Freiburg, Germany, on 8 February 1909. He died in Concord, California on 24 February 1999, and is buried in the Orthodox Jewish Cemetery, 4712 Fairfax Avenue, Oakland, California.[1]

---

[*] President Emeritus of Manchester Community College, Manchester, Connecticut; Interim President of Middlesex Community College, Middletown, Connecticut; President of the University of Aberdeen Development Trust USA. In putting together what follows, I received significant help from my wife Linda Daube, my brothers Ben and Michael Daube, my son Matthew Daube, DD's second wife Helen Smelser Daube, her daughter Tina Smelser, my cousin Jacob (Bubi) Daube, David Carey Miller, Calum Carmichael, Paul du Plessis, Ed Epstein, Sue Forteath, Bill Gordon, David Ibbetson, Bernard Jackson, Ephraim Karnafogel, Andrew Lewis, Mike Meston, Marion Paterson, Alan Rodger, Lord Sacks, Brian Simpson, Paul Slack, Kathleen Vanden Heuvel, Ken Walters and Reuven Yaron. It is to be feared that errors and infelicities are my own.

[1] My purpose here is not to write a life or a belated obituary. See, in particular, Alan Rodger's superb and definitive biography: 'David Daube (8.2.1909 – 24.2.1999)', *Zeitschrift der Savigny-Stiftung für Rechtsgeschichte* (rom. Abt.), 118 (2001), XIV–LII; also by Alan Rodger: 'David Daube (1909–1999)', in J. Beatson and R. Zimmermann, eds., *Jurists Uprooted: German-speaking Émigré Lawyers in Twentieth-century Britain* (Oxford 2004), 233–48; 'Law for All Times: The Work and Contribution of David Daube', in E. Metzger, ed., *Law for All Times: Essays in Memory of David Daube* [*Roman Legal Tradition*, 2] (Lawrence, KS, 2004), 3–23. See also the work of Calum Carmichael of Cornell University, and the website put together by Kathleen Vanden Heuvel of Boalt Hall, the University of California at Berkeley ('David Daube', hosted at Boalt Hall).

When I was a small boy, in 1947, he wrote an article entitled *Did Macedo Murder His Father?*[2] He began, 'I'm afraid that he did.' But F. S. Marsh, Lady Margaret's Professor of Divinity at Cambridge, made him change it to 'It is to be feared that he did.' Years later, when I was studying for an honours degree in English at Aberdeen, we agreed that this was misplaced advice: the less formal version was better. It is in that spirit that what follows is informal. Some of it was used at an after-dinner speech at DD's hundredth birthday celebration at King's College, The University of Aberdeen, in February, 2009.

* * *

David Daube's three sons have lived for more than a quarter of a century in Massachusetts and Connecticut; Toronto, Ontario; and Perth, Western Australia.[3] We were all born in Cambridge, England: 1937 (Jonathan Mahram), 1946 (Benjamin Jeremy) and 1948 (Michael Matthew). Referring to the utility scheme for buying furniture that existed in the United Kingdom from 1942 to 1952, DD would refer to me as the Prewar child and my brothers as the Utility babies. Between us, DD and we three had citizenship in four countries, and passports to match. (DD never bothered with American citizenship, retaining the British passport he had had since the

---

(Alan Rodger was DD's last doctoral student at Oxford before he left for the United States, while Kathleen was, in manifold ways, the daughter that DD never had.) See also T. Honoré, 'Daube, David (1909–1999)', in *Oxford Dictionary of National Biography* (Oxford 2004); D. Nörr, 'Nachrufe David Daube', in *Jahrbuch 1999* [Jahrbücher der Bayerischen Akademie der Wissenschaften] (Munich 2000), 264–70; Peter Stein's obituaries in *The Caian: The Magazine of Gonville and Caius College*, (November 1999), 151–54; and 'David Daube 1909-1999', in *2000 Lectures and Memoirs* [*Proceedings of the British Academy*, 111] (Oxford 2001), 428–44; and Kathleen Vanden Heuvel, Laurent Mayali and John Noonan, 'Professor David Daube: A Tribute', *California Law Review*, 87 (1999), 1051–58.

[2] *Zeitschrift der Savigny-Stiftung für Rechtsgeschichte* (rom. Abt.), 65 (1947), 261.

[3] Benjamin Jeremy Daube, now retired from TV production at the Canadian Broadcasting Corporation (CBC-TV), is a consultant in Toronto, Ontario. Michael Matthew Daube is Professor and Director of the Public Health Advocacy Institute at Curtin University of Technology, Perth, Western Australia.

end of the war. Buckland vouched for him.) Despite huge distances and air fares to match, the brothers are close and get together relatively frequently.

Michael, a superb bureaucrat, decreed that the centenary of DD's birth should be celebrated, and promptly delegated the task of organizing this to me. Fortunately, David Carey Miller, Emeritus Professor of Property Law and former Head of the School of Law at the University of Aberdeen, offered to put together a conference. Suffice it to say that the event he made happen would have pleased DD enormously and turned out to be a wondrous mixture of appropriate academic rigour and a reunion of DD's family, former doctoral students and disciples. It would be impossible to exaggerate David Carey Miller's skill in bringing a disparate crowd together and ensuring the happiness of all. I cannot overstate our thanks to him for organizing something that family and friends will treasure for a very long time. The brothers felt confirmed in our decision of 2002 to give DD's papers to the University of Aberdeen.

My self-assigned task was to prepare some after-dinner remarks that would add to people's knowledge about DD, that would keep the well-fed company awake for twenty-five minutes or so, and that would be of interest to people who had known DD exceedingly well (e.g. Alan Rodger[4] and Reuven Yaron[5]) as well as those who had never met him. I wanted, in particular, to paint a picture of a person who had an amazing range of attributes and interests — and who was not always easy. As DD's grandson Matthew put it at the University of Aberdeen, 'David was a different man in different places to different people.'

So I took a leaf out of my wife's book. She is a creator of lists, and I made four. Here goes.

---

[4] The Right Honourable the Lord Rodger of Earlsferry; Justice of the Supreme Court of the United Kingdom.
[5] Professor Emeritus, Hebrew University of Jerusalem.

1. Six men who could intimidate DD

Yes, all men; he was, after all, born before World War One. Not a large number (DD was not easily intimidated) but two of them were from his Aberdeen years (1951–1955).

OTTO LENEL. Born in 1849, Lenel fought against France in 1870–1871 and then became a professor at the University of Strassburg, which was then in Germany, moving to the University of Freiburg in 1907. (The Albert-Ludwigs-Universität Freiburg was founded in 1457, less than four decades before the University of Aberdeen.) He was already an octogenarian when DD, sixty years younger, became his student. Lenel died of a broken heart in 1935; although he was not practising, according to the Nazis, he was as Jewish as DD. At some point in the thirties, his daughter Bertha sold 6,500 of his books to Louisiana State University. (They are not now separately catalogued, but they are still there.) Today, there is a plaque on his house at Holbeinstrasse 5, Freiburg, which is about six minutes' walk from where DD and his family lived (Goethestrasse 35). As Alan Rodger documents, Lenel recommended DD to Herbert F. Jolowicz, who was then at University College, London.[6] He, in turn, sent him on to Buckland. (Jolowicz went on to Oxford and was DD's immediate predecessor.)

WILLIAM WARWICK BUCKLAND. Regius Professor of Civil Law at Cambridge from 1914 to 1945 and President (second only to the Master) of Gonville and Caius College, it was Buckland to whom DD went, penniless, in 1933. DD spoke no English, Buckland spoke little or no German, so they conversed initially in French. Buckland made DD read Shakespeare and Dickens, and DD earned his Cambridge Ph.D. in 1936. (It must have been Buckland's influence: DD would always stress the importance of original texts; and he would say that all you needed to know was the Bible and Shakespeare.) I

---

[6] Rodger, 'David Daube (1909–1999)' (note 1), 234.

remember when Buckland died in 1946: he was cremated on a Saturday and DD, an orthodox Jew at the time, walked to the Cambridge crematorium, which is over five miles from the centre of town. NB: I don't think Buckland and Lenel ever met; but they hang together, with DD between them, on the wall in the chambers of Alan Rodger at the newly established Supreme Court of the United Kingdom in London.

SIR ARNOLD MCNAIR, who became Lord McNair in 1955. A professor of international law, then comparative law, at Cambridge in the days when a professor really was a professor, he was Vice-Chancellor of the University of Liverpool from 1937 to 1945 and played a key role in bringing DD back to the mainland when he was interned for a short time as an 'enemy alien' on the Isle of Man. (McNair went on to be a judge at the International Court of Justice at The Hague and then first President of the European Court of Human Rights at Strasbourg.) I recall being told, quite sternly, by both parents to behave when we went for tea at the McNairs' place in Eltisley, about eleven miles west of Cambridge: soon after, DD became a university lecturer, so I suppose it was some kind of job interview.[7]

PRINCIPAL SIR THOMAS TAYLOR, who brought DD to Aberdeen. A tall, stern, imposing and moral figure, he did not encourage relaxation. A set of lectures he gave at the University of Durham was entitled *The Discipline of Virtue*.[8]

SIR JAMES ROBERTSON, Rector of the Aberdeen Grammar School. It was Sir James who, seeing how dysfunctional my parents' marriage had already become, somehow got me to skip the sixth form and go to the University of Aberdeen at the age of fifteen. 'Now, professor', he would say . . . and DD would not argue. (Four years later, having graduated in

---

[7] A pleasant coincidence: the consultant for the new University of Aberdeen Library was Dr Alice Prochaska, McNair's granddaughter, Yale Librarian and about to become Principal of Somerville College, Oxford, in 2010.

[8] See T. M. Taylor, *The Discipline of Virtue: Reflections on Law and Liberty* (London 1954).

English, I went to the Institute of Education at the University of London on my way to becoming a teacher. I returned to Aberdeen for a few days, in part, to brag to Sir James about my accomplishments. Even though I was working in highly selective grammar schools at the time, I was captivated by the comprehensive school movement and was telling him about a paper I had just written. 'But you know', I said, 'there's a Scottish report that's really good and that no one in England seems to know about.' 'Oh', he said, 'you like it?' And he pulled the manuscript out of a desk drawer: he had written it himself.)

UNIFORMED POLICEMEN. Shortly after DD was appointed to his chair at Aberdeen, he and I were cycling near the Catholic Church in Cambridge, and he sailed through a traffic light. When stopped by a policeman, he declared, 'I am a professor of law', and got off.

2. Ten men on the world stage with whom DD had real conversations

Yes, all men (again). In most cases, I have little idea what they talked about, but I take DD at his word.

POPE PIUS XII. I do not know when or where they met. Pacelli was nuncio in Bavaria and then Germany before becoming Pope in 1939.

NIELS BOHR, the Danish physicist and Nobel laureate. They met in 1943, immediately after Bohr had been flown out of Denmark and had passed out during the flight, not having put on his oxygen equipment.

LEE KWAN YEW, Prime Minister of Singapore for over thirty years, who earned a double starred First Class Honours degree in law after the Second World War and was a student of DD's.

ABBA EBAN, who was a student at Cambridge when he was still Aubrey Eban. (He earned a triple first and was fluent in ten languages.) Even when he was Israel's Foreign Minister, our mother, recalling Cambridge afternoon teas for Jewish students, would refer to him as 'little Aubrey'.

MARTIN BUBER, who received the degree of Doctor of Divinity from the University of Aberdeen in 1953. One of my brothers asked him whether he slept with his beard under or outside the sheets. (Brother Michael swears it was I; but how would he know?) The product of an orthodox Jewish home, I was shocked that he and his wife left Aberdeen on a Saturday afternoon train.

PRIME MINISTER AND OXFORD CHANCELLOR HAROLD MACMILLAN. When the Regius Chair of Civil Law at Cambridge fell vacant, there was talk of switching its remit from Roman law to modern European law. (In those days, Oxbridge regius professors were appointed by the Queen, upon the recommendation of the Prime Minister. Nowadays, the University has a strong recommending role.) DD took the train for London and headed straight for 10 Downing Street — without an appointment. Somehow, he got to see his Chancellor[9] and persuaded him that the European Community would be upset if Cambridge were perceived to be devaluing Roman law. Nothing more was heard of any possible changes, and Peter Stein, who had succeeded DD as Professor of Jurisprudence at Aberdeen, got the job, which he held from 1968 to 1993. To this day, both Oxford and Cambridge regius professors of civil law are Roman lawyers. This was DD's first and last foray into politics.

HARRY TRUMAN. President Truman received an honorary doctorate from Oxford on 20 June 1956, and there is a picture of him and DD smiling together. Historians have opined that

---

[9] Note that in the United Kingdom and many Commonwealth countries, the titular head of the university is the chancellor, while the vice-chancellor is what Americans would call the president and Scots call the principal.

that degree meant a great deal to Truman, who, though very well read, did not have a college degree and, besides, was still under considerable attack, especially from academics, for dropping two atomic bombs on Japan.

JAWAHARLAL NEHRU, first and longest-serving Prime Minister of India. DD told me that Nehru's name came up for Chancellor of the University of Cambridge in 1950. But they weren't ready for a person of colour, and the honour went to Marshall of the Royal Air Force Lord Tedder. When DD went round the world in the early sixties, he was entertained to dinner by Nehru, who spoke with him about the difficulty of bringing up a daughter.

SARVEPALLI RADHAKRISHNAN, the second President of India, who had been Spalding Professor of Eastern Religions at Oxford and was a Fellow of All Souls College.

WALTER MONDALE, who entertained DD to dinner while he was Vice President of the United States. DD's widow Helen tells me that he asked Joan Mondale for the recipe of her yogurt dessert.

3. Seventeen matters in which DD had (or feigned) no interest

DRIVING. Actually, he did drive a car into a ditch in Germany in the thirties and promptly gave up driving. (That was his story!) In Cambridge days (1933–1951) both my parents had bicycles and used them. If you google 'Sunbeam, bicycles', you will see images of the bicycle DD would ride to his lectures.

HOSPITALS. Can't blame him. When he was growing up, hospitals were where you went to die. He never saw them any differently.

SMOKING. DD was a smoker until Dr Harry Richards, our family doctor, told him to stop in the late thirties or early forties. I remember up to a hundred cigarettes lying around for guests at my parents' sherry parties in Cambridge; brother Ben recalls a rack of pipes on the mantelpiece in Aberdeen. How the culture has changed.

THE TELEPHONE. When, after World War Two, we got a telephone at 29 Chesterton Hall Crescent, Cambridge, DD insisted that the number not be published in the directory. And one time, he threw the phone out of the window. Years later, when he was in his office at Berkeley, he would be devilishly hard to reach. Matthew, his grandson, got into the practice of making two calls: first to Kathleen Vanden Heuvel, who would let DD know when he was going to get a call; then at the appointed time. When she cleared out his office, she found innumerable scraps of paper stating, 'Matthew will call you at x o'clock.' Michael remembers him shouting into the phone.

NEWSPAPERS. When I was growing up, my maternal grandparents, who lived in the house until August 1946, read the *Manchester Guardian* (now *The Guardian*) and would sometimes read the *News Chronicle*, which went out of business in 1960. Not DD. Bill Gordon[10] reports that, in his Aberdeen days, DD told his students that he read the (Aberdeen) *Evening Express* (daily) and *The Observer* (Sundays).[11] In his last decades, he bought the *San Francisco Chronicle* almost every day, and especially enjoyed the crossword.[12]

ACADEMIC ADMINISTRATION. He successfully avoided ever being a dean or a department chair. When he had a secretary (Mrs MacBean in Aberdeen and Mrs Segal in his early years at Berkeley; no one at Cambridge or Oxford), he didn't quite know what to do with her. (Mrs Segal did a lot of filing.) When I became a college president in 1978, he expressed bewilderment about what I really did. He came to my inauguration in 1988 and, representing the University of Oxford, led the academic procession. 'Do I have to speak?' 'No.' Mat-

---

[10] Douglas Professor of Civil Law Emeritus, University of Glasgow.
[11] See above, page 94.
[12] See below, page 166.

thew writes, 'He took pride in having mucked up some of his tasks at Oxford, to such an extent that some duties (e.g. presiding over exams) were removed from the regius professor.'

Ken Walters, now retired from the University of Washington, was a student of DD's at Berkeley. He wrote to me as follows:

> I think DD was unusually shrewd in figuring out that he could be far happier and more productive if he didn't complicate his life with certain things, including the sink hole of one's time that is administration. There is no doubt at all in my mind that he could have done the administrative thing had he wanted to. He clearly knew what it took, and made a decision that it was not what he wanted to do with his time, or his reputation. But was he tempted?[13]

I disagree totally with the above, but wonder what others think.

FILING PAPERS. My sympathies to the people who are going through the DD papers at the University of Aberdeen. Making life easy for others was not always his prime goal in life.

WRITING BOOK REVIEWS. He'd always praise, never criticize; realized that, on the whole, writing such book reviews was a waste of time. Reuven Yaron, who knows DD the academic better than I, begs to disagree.

WRITING TESTIMONIALS/LETTERS OF REFERENCE. Again, they'd always be over the top and therefore worthless. I would argue with him about this (and got nowhere).

After reading the above couple of sentences, Brian Simpson[14] e-mailed me:

> You may like to know one other quirk of your father. He could I think never bring himself to write negative letters of recommendation for jobs, so he adopted the practice of writing very positive ones. But after sending them he was, I think, worried over his obligation to be honest and mention the downside as well as the upside. So the letter would always be followed by a phone call along the lines of 'I should perhaps have mentioned that X holds idiotic views about Y (or has recently killed a pupil or whatever).' I always

---

[13] See C. Carmichael, ed., *The Jottings of David Daube* (New York 2008), 51.
[14] Charles F. and Edith J. Clyne Professor of Law, University of Michigan, and honorary fellow of Lincoln College, Oxford.

found this endearing. At the end of the day by combining the letter and the phone call you got a reliable assessment.

MODERN SPOKEN HEBREW. His command of classical Hebrew was, of course, superb. When he was offered the first chair of Roman law by the Hebrew University in 1949 or 1950, I thought he declined because my mother had had an understandable nervous breakdown; maybe it was, in part, because he wouldn't have been able to lecture in modern Hebrew (at least, not immediately). Kathleen Vanden Heuvel has a different take. DD told her many times that he did not agree with the premise of Hebrew University, although he respected many of the people there. (Sounds *ex post facto* to me, even though I do remember him never having been a Zionist.)

RADIO AND TELEVISION. Professing absolutely no interest. My grandparents had a radio, where they would listen to the nine o'clock news, but we did not have one, even during the War. When, on the way to and from the Cambridge synagogue, we would pass Ward's, a TV shop near Milton Road Corner and the Tivoli Cinema where I first saw *The Third Man*, DD would point out how the screens were flickering. He did broadcast on the BBC Third Programme (now transmogrified into Radio Three) on Humpty Dumpty,[15] and Ben recalls much commotion. And before his world tour, he and Ben learned the rudiments of Russian from a BBC series. In his rare television interviews he performed superbly. My wife Linda reminds me that there was a television set in one of the homes he lived in during his last decade: the Jerry Springer Show left him totally bemused.

COOKING (as opposed to eating). Brother Ben recalls, 'When we returned from a couple of weeks in Broadstairs, Kent [where DD's sister-in-law Helen lived] in 1957 or thereabouts, piled on the kitchen counter to Herta's horror were two dozen egg shells. No frying pan had been used. They had to have been cooked somehow.' Years later, the kitchen in his apartment in Konstanz was a disaster. Brother Michael writes,

---

[15] See the text accompanying notes 36–37 below.

'When we visited, the kitchen sink contained a long-abandoned coffee percolator that had failed to work properly. Somebody hadn't told him that coffee beans should be ground.' Linda remembers him telling her with pride how he had learned to boil water to make instant coffee.

ELECTRIC (OR ELECTRONIC) TYPEWRITERS. He had his ancient portable, and that was good enough for him. Alan Rodger, in a letter to me, called it 'disreputable'.

COMPUTERS. Absolutely no comprehension. I took him to the Berkeley main library one time and showed him his name in the catalogue: vaguely interested and totally bemused. He would have been quite befuddled had he seen me google 'David Daube' and get 51,700 results, or go to books.google.com and find 581 references to him and 31 to his brother Benjamin.

PRACTICAL MATTERS. DD did put his toe in the water: he was admitted to Gray's Inn on 28 July 1938, but, as my informant put it, 'Like many academic lawyers, he was not called to the Bar.' And I can't imagine him standing in line to register during the War.[16]

MONEY. When DD went to Cambridge in 1933, he had no money. He happened to be in Germany during the Währungsreform of 1948, when the Deutsche Mark replaced the Reichsmark. When my cousin Mike Austin and his wife Sue helped me clean out his room at the Berkeley City Club we found a suitcase under the bed. In that suitcase were American, Australian and Canadian dollars, Deutschmarks (most of them outdated), and British pounds. Tina and I took them to DD's Wells Fargo Bank; they amounted to a few thousand dollars. And he continued to worry about his suitcase. To me, it meant that he never quite got over his fear of being a refugee again: he was ready to flee at a moment's notice. And yet, as many of my readers will know, he didn't bother to

---

[16] I still remember my identity card number: TACY 15:3. My parents' were TACY 15:1 and 2.

negotiate an appropriate salary when he left Oxford for Boalt Hall. And his restaurant tips were ridiculously generous.[17] Towards the end of his life, he signed the documents that would allow me to make his end-of-life decisions, but he never signed away the authority to manage his checkbook. Deep, deep down, he may have been more afraid of losing his money than his life.

MARKING/GRADING ON THE (BELL) CURVE, i.e. having to give a certain percentage of students in each class As, Bs, Cs, etc. This was mandatory at Boalt Hall during his glory days. He opposed. He got nowhere.

4. Seventy-seven aspects of DD

Yes, this is a long list. I welcome readers' additions and editorial comments. These 'aspects', some trivial and some not, are hopefully not just gossipy tidbits; rather, they are meant to help understand DD. He was nothing if not complex, and he didn't make it easy for those who knew and/or loved him.

NINETEEN HUNDRED AND NINE. Before World War One. Von Bülow handed over as German Chancellor to von Bethmann-Hollweg; Asquith was British Prime Minister; Theodore Roosevelt was the American President. DD was born the same year as Isaiah Berlin, Victor Borge, Barry Goldwater, Ernst Gombrich, Andrei Gromyko, Kwame Nkrumah, U Thant and Simone Weil: he knew some of them. And that year Isaac Albéniz, Geronimo, George Meredith and Algernon Charles Swinburne all died: he knew none of them — whatever he may have told you. More importantly, Germany was then the centre of the academic world: when Sigmund Freud lectured that year at Clark University in Worcester, Massachusetts, he spoke in German, sans translator, it being assumed that

---

[17] See below, page 177.

the assembled academics would all understand.

✦

HIS WET NURSE MINNA. When his mother realized that he preferred Minna to her, Minna was abruptly fired. This was an issue for DD for the rest of his life.

✦

TONSILS. When he was a small boy, he had his tonsils removed without anesthetic. Another good reason for his lifelong hatred of hospitals. Upon reading this, Peter Hennock, Emeritus Professor of History at Liverpool and a cousin of my mother's, wrote:

> I too had my tonsils removed in Germany without any anesthetic when I was quite a small boy. I was given to understand later when I mentioned this in England that in Germany tonsils were not totally cut out as was the case in England and probably the U.S.A. It was the tips full of pus that were removed with clippers. But what a painful experience!

✦

SCHOOLBOY PRANKS. When I was a child, DD would entertain me with tales of pranks he had played when he was in his teens. I can't remember a single one. But Ben writes, 'At his parents' first party after they moved to a barely completed house (35 Goethestrasse, Freiburg), the brothers put a sign up outside the house warning the guests that "Die Toiletten befinden sich gegenüber dem Münster" [The toilets are opposite the Cathedral].' That would have been a kilometre's walk away! DD's playfulness remained throughout his life. Mike Meston, now Emeritus Professor of Scots Law at Aberdeen, tells a delightful tale from the Roman Law class of 1954–1955,[18] of which he was a member:

> I regret that I am unable to claim responsibility for the furniture rearrangement, but it was certainly someone from our enormous class of about sixteen students. I have never discovered who actually did it. When David came in to the small classroom in St. Mary's [the building that contained the law school at that time, now housing archaeology, geography and land economy],

---

[18] The ordinary class: see Professor Gordon's remarks above, pages 91–98.

the desk had been turned to face the blackboard and the chair or stool was now out in front, also facing the blackboard. David didn't even pause, and simply sat down facing away from us and began to address the blackboard. ... There was no problem about somewhere to place his notes, since he used only something like a postcard with a few headings on it. ... There was no reference to furniture alterations ... in the questions in the subsequent Roman Law examinations, unlike the Scots Law exams which tended to include difficult problems involving goldfish after a goldfish materialized in T. B. Smith's glass of water on the desk.[19]

Ten years after DD's death, his grandson Matthew commented on his 'extraordinary sense of humor':

During one of my visits to California, he was taken by ambulance to a hospital from the nursing home. His second wife Helen and her daughter Tina rushed to his side, as did I. We encountered David lying on a stretcher in the middle of the emergency room, waiting for the doctor, his eyes closed. To break the tension, naturally, after a few minutes I accused him of having faked the whole episode just to get the four of us together. He opened his eyes, looked up, and gave a taste of his infamous smile. Even in those moments, he treasured his reputation as a troublemaker.

Matthew went on to describe another hospital incident:

We went to the cafeteria to await some of the testing results, both of us near exhaustion, David from being in his eighties, and me from being twenty years old and taking care of a grandparent who was in his eighties. Wearily, I headed off to the toilets, and returned to find David still at the table, but my drink was gone. That drink vanishing felt like the last straw in a very long and arduous day. I felt ready to give up, and then David, again with a smile, lifted up the drink from the chair next to him, where he had hidden it. He handed it to me with the glee of a magician conjuring a rabbit out of mid-air.

VERBAL PLAYFULNESS. During his penultimate visit to New England, flying in to lecture at Harvard, my wife Linda, in an attempt to get below the surface, asked DD to describe his (notional) third wife. (I hasten to add that DD had no intent to 'go there'.) 'Well', he said, 'the first two will have been HErta and HElen, so the third would have to be HEnrietta.' And, of course, the third would have to be beautiful and Jewish.

---

[19] Smith was DD's closest colleague during his Aberdeen days: Professor of Scots Law and Dean of the Faculty of Law. He went on to the University of Edinburgh in 1958, and was later knighted. See Professor MacQueen's paper above, pages 11–36.

JOKES. DD's favourite joke as I was growing up: a Cambridge student who had had too much to drink relieved himself at St Botolph's Church, which is on Trumpington Street at the junction with Silver Street. He was caught, presumably by a proctor, and 'sent down', i.e. dismissed from the University. He had, up to that point, done nothing wrong, so asked his tutor for a letter of reference. His tutor supposedly wrote, 'Mr X leaves the University without a stain on his character, though not without some on the Church of Saint Botolph.' DD told me this one several times. His favourite German joke was his claim that the great German poet Heine wanted to have the following words carved on his tombstone:

> Hier liegen meine Gebeine;
> Ich wollt' es wären Deine,
> Heinrich Heine

('Here lie my bones; I wish they were yours.' Tacky thought, but the German rhymes.)

Britain's Chief Rabbi, Lord Sacks, marked Shakespeare's birthday in 2010, 23 April, by calling me from London to tell me of the one time he met DD, at Caius College, Cambridge, in 1968. He told me the philosophers' joke that DD had recounted . . . forty-two years before:

Ludwig Wittgenstein, Elizabeth Anscombe and Herbert Hart, renowned philosophers in their day, were at the Oxford train station. They were so engrossed in their conversation that they failed to notice the London train steaming in and about to leave. As it was about to depart, Hart managed to jump on, as did Anscombe . . . 'an ENORMOUS woman' [Sacks trying and failing to mimic DD's accent]. Wittgenstein was distraught. Someone came up to console him: 'There's another train in an hour.' Wittgenstein: 'Yes, yes, but *they* came to see *me* off.'

Lord Sacks went on to tell me that DD told him that as he aged and his audiences diminished, he increased the rate at which he would tell indiscreet stories about his colleagues.

It became clear to me that the Chief Rabbi knows DD's work. He referred to *Studies in Biblical Law*.[20] And the Gifford Lectures. He mentioned DD's sixpenny bet, that Mar-

---

[20] I remember going with my father to the Cambridge University Press on Trumpington Street to deliver the manuscript. I must have been nine.

lowe would have turned out an even better writer than Shakespeare had he lived. DD, said the Chief Rabbi, 'had an extraordinary imagination and was wildly speculative.'

⁂

MATZOCOFFEE. A ghastly concoction that only DD could love. Crumble matzo into a large coffee cup or a cereal bowl and add coffee (with or without milk and sugar); eat with a spoon; persuade one of your sons to join you.

⁂

KAISERSCHMARRN (Emperor's mishmash). A light caramelized pancake, this was DD's favourite dessert.

⁂

BADEN. Baden, a grand duchy when DD was born, existed from the early twelfth century until after the Second World War. DD enjoyed opposing its merger and the creation of Baden-Württemberg in 1952, especially since few took him seriously. When he got his honorary LL.D. at Cambridge, the Chancellor, the Duke of Edinburgh, and he chatted about Prince Max of Baden and the Schule Schloss Salem, which he (the Duke) had attended for two terms before accompanying Kurt Hahn, the founding headmaster, to Gordonstoun in Scotland. (NB: there were about 1,140 Jews in Freiburg in the thirties.)

⁂

FIFTH ZIONIST CONGRESS. Basel, 1901. The family still has a picture that was given to all attendees, and DD told me that his father Jakob had been there. Attempts to confirm this, including correspondence with the Central Zionist Archives in Jerusalem, have failed; there is no listing of attendees at the Fifth Congress. In Cambridge days, DD would hang up the picture in our sukkah every year; his granddaughter Katharine now has it up on her living room wall.

⁂

BROTHER BENNI. All his life, DD worshipped his older brother (born 23 March 1902, so about seven years older than DD), declaring that Benni was by far the more accomplished of the two.[21] Benni, who would be described today as ultraorthodox for most of his life, studied in Berlin with Alexander Altmann.[22] By the time I was born (1937), Benni had tuberculosis; exactly when he acquired this I do not know. In the foreword to his book, he refers to 'mehrjährige schwere Krankheit' (heavy illness for many years). Since he was a Jew, his 1938 book, *Zu den Rechtsproblemen in Aischylos' Agamemnon*, had to be published outside Germany.[23] The foreword is dated 23 November, my first birthday. Benni took his doctoral examinations at the University of Basel on 28 May 1937, and was officially granted his doctorate in 1939, after publication of his book. (The Staatsarchiv des Kantons Basel-Stadt have sent me a copy of his file. Amazing to me that it was lying there all these years.) Somehow, DD was able to get him out of Germany as well as their parents and his (DD's) parents-in-law. It was in England that Benni met my beloved aunt Helen, née O'Callaghan, who broke off an engagement to marry him. There is a piece in the London *Daily Mirror* of 10 September 1943, entitled 'Taken to Wedding on Stretcher'. (By this time Benni had become a communist, moving from one orthodoxy to another.) Benni died on 23 March 1946, and is buried in Nottingham. My brother Ben, who was born just over five months after his death, is named after him.

∽

MAHRAM OF ROTHENBURG. Supposedly, my brothers and I are descended through DD's mother Selma from this thirteenth-

---

[21] The University of Aberdeen has a trove of letters from Benni to DD and my mother.
[22] Altmann left Germany in 1938 to become Communal Rabbi in Manchester, England. In 1959 he moved to a chair at Brandeis University, living in Newton Center, Massachusetts, until his death in 1987. Neither my brother Ben nor I knew anything of this when we both lived in the Boston area in the sixties; ironically, I taught at Newton High School from 1963 to 1965 and worked for the Newton Public Schools in 1967–1968.
[23] Zürich: Max Niehans, 1938.

century rabbi, who is buried in Worms.[24] There is a tradition that there will always be a Daube male with the name Mahram; so my great-uncle Max Ascher[25] died in 1936, I was born in 1937, and my second name is Mahram. I have informed all DD's six grandchildren of my hope that, after my death, the next descendant, male or female, be named Mahram.

⁂

SONS AND GRANDCHILDREN. DD would have readily agreed when I described him at his funeral as a rotten husband (to his first wife) and an overpowering father. But something happened in his last three decades, and he became a loving, caring, accepting and generous grandfather. As anyone who goes through his papers at the University of Aberdeen will discover, he kept every card, every scrap of paper that any of his six grandchildren sent him. He had frank and intimate conversations with some of them that he would probably not have had with his sons. Matthew and he became especially close, with Matthew becoming, to some degree, his caregiver in his declining years. At the Aberdeen gathering, he spoke of the respect DD showed for others, especially his grandchildren. He said:

My sister Katharine recalls . . . respect and the tremendous acceptance she received from David when she first came out as a lesbian, even though he did take care to accompany this acceptance with the pronouncement that he was 100% heterosexual.

---

[24] See S. L. Gilman and J. Zipes, *Yale Companion to Jewish Writing and Thought in German Culture 1096–1996* (New Haven, CN, 1997), 27–34 (Ephraim Kanarfogel on R. Meir ben Barukh (Maharam) of Rothenburg). I recently had a helpful e-mail from Professor Karnarfogel, who is the E. Billi Ivry Professor of Jewish History in the Bernard Revel Graduate School of Jewish Studies at Yeshiva University, New York City; he knows DD's work. He assured me that there is no significant difference between 'Mahram' and 'Maharam'. At the Aberdeen dinner, I declared that I wished someone could dig him up, test his DNA and see if he really is our ancestor. Poor taste, perhaps, but DD would have enjoyed the thought.

[25] Max's daughter Ruth Ascher, DD's first cousin, still lives in Caversham, Reading. She is a pianist who taught at the University of Reading for many years; a pupil of the great pianist Solomon. She is the only person left who has memories of DD and his brother as youngsters.

Needless to say, he would have been over the moon had he lived to see a great-granddaughter and twin great-grandsons. If anyone had told me when I was growing up that DD would become a 'family man', I would have snorted with disdain.

~

THE TALMUD. Of course. DD had a set in his study at home in Cambridge, and he used it.

When David Patterson, President Emeritus of the Oxford Centre of Hebrew and Jewish Studies, died in 2005, Raymond Dwek, then head of the Department of Biochemistry at Oxford, spoke:

> I well remember [Patterson] in the Choolant Society [cholent, as it is usually spelled, a traditional Jewish stew simmered overnight and eaten for lunch on the Sabbath] in the late 60s and early 70s. Every society was required by University rules to have one senior member and there was always confusion as to whether for the Choolant Society this was David Daube, Professor of Roman Law or David Patterson as either could have been the senior member! At successive termly dinners first one David then the other would give a scholarly discourse using Talmudic and biblical precedents to show why he was the clear choice of senior member. The wit and scholarship were humbling to behold and we all felt tremendously privileged to be in the same company as these two outstanding scholars.

Small world: David Patterson had written DD's obituary for *The Guardian* in 1999.[26]

~

LITURGICAL SINGING; OR CANTILLATION. In his Cambridge days, DD enjoyed leading services, using much that he had learned in the Betsaal in Freiburg as well as adaptations of early Western music.[27] I remember the time (it must have been in the forties) when Rabbi Ehrentreu, who had married my parents in Munich in 1936 and who had just returned from internment in Australia, was Choson Torah and DD was Choson Bereishis. (The former is the person completing the

---

[26] D. Patterson, 'Professor David Daube', *The Guardian* (12 March 1999).
[27] See W. Frankel and H. Miller, eds., *Gown and Tallith: In Commemoration of the Fiftieth Anniversary of the Founding of the Cambridge University Jewish Society* (London 1989), especially 25, 61, 75, 76 and 105–22.

annual cycle of Torah reading on the festival known as Simchas Torah; the latter is the person who begins the new cycle. The former is usually senior to the latter: remember that DD was in his forties.)

∽

TRAVEL. Yes, he enjoyed travel. But he never set foot on the African continent. After my family and I had spent 1968–1970 at the University of Malawi, he would quip that he was leaving Africa to me. He was pleased that his older granddaughter was born in Malawi and has a Malawian birth certificate.

∽

VERONA. DD always had a soft spot for Verona, site of his first postwar conference. He enjoyed receiving letters addressed to "Illustrissime Professore!"

∽

BIROBIDZHAN. DD was intrigued by the Jewish Autonomous District, five thousand miles east of Moscow and near the Chinese border, that was planned in the late twenties, supposedly as a national homeland for Soviet Jewry. It was officially created in 1934 and soon made to suffer, beginning with purges in 1936. Birobidzhan is on the Trans-Siberian Railway, and I think DD visited and made some contacts there when he went round the world after Michael's bar mitzvah.

∽

PARIS. DD loved Paris, and the honorary doctorate from the Sorbonne meant a huge amount. Benni's widow Helen, who spoke perfect French, accompanied him on that trip.

∽

LANGUAGES. My best estimate is that he was proficient in at least eleven languages. I have heard tell of as many as fourteen: English, German, French, Italian, Spanish, classical Hebrew, Aramaic, Latin, Greek, Russian, Sanskrit (at Göttingen, his teacher was Friedrich Carl Andreas), possibly Icelandic. In Berkeley, I asked him in which language he thought. The answer, which shouldn't have surprised me but did: English.

ACCENT. Like Henry Kissinger, DD retained his German accent. (Supposedly Kissinger's brother Walter speaks accentless English.) DD told his grandson Matthew that his wife Herta had sent him to an English accent coach. He did go — once!

SPEAKING GERMAN. During the War, DD insisted on speaking German both in- and outside the house, which increasingly aggravated my mother as the years went on. Imagine my discomfort on the streets of Cambridge. In her book *Continental Britons: German-Jewish Refugees from Nazi Germany*,[28] Marion Berghahn writes:

> The German-Jewish Aid Committee, an Anglo-Jewish foundation, published a brochure, probably at the beginning of the War, entitled *While you are in England: Helpful Information and Guidance for every Refugee*. It contained eight 'commandments' to teach the refugees good behavior so as not to provoke any animosity. Thus they were asked to 'refrain from speaking German in the streets and in public conveyances and in public places such as restaurants. Talk halting English rather than fluent German.'

---

[28] M. Berghahn, *Continental Britons: German-Jewish Refugees from Nazi Germany*, rev. ed. (Oxford and New York 2007), 139–40. The Association of Jewish Refugees borrowed the title of Berghahn's book for a 2002 exhibit 'Continental Britons: Jewish Refugees from Nazi Europe' (viewable from the AJR website). In that year my wife Linda found the exhibit by accident, forced onto the streets of Camden Town by an Underground strike, and deciding to enter the Jewish Museum there. On the walls of the exhibit there was a listing of the most distinguished of the 60,000 or so refugees (Sigmund Freud, for example) and there, in big print, was 'David Daube'.

ATTITUDE TOWARDS GERMANS. Immediately after the War, DD reconnected with people in Germany. I remember my mother's distress when he invited Johannes Hempel (who had been one of his teachers at the University of Göttingen but had become an early and enthusiastic member of the Nazi party), not only to come to Cambridge but to stay with us at 29 Chesterton Hall Crescent. Hempel was a signatory to the 1933 commitment of professors at German universities and colleges to Adolf Hitler and the Nazi state (*Bekenntnis der Professoren an den deutschen Universitäten und Hochschulen zu Adolf Hitler und dem nationalsozialistischen Staat*). DD reminds me of Yehudi Menuhin, who visited Germany and played at concentration camps, but also played for Herbert von Karajan in the forties.

GRAVITAS. DD's second wife Helen points out that there was always a presence. She's right. For sure, he spoke in uninterruptable paragraphs.

PIANO. DD was quite a good pianist. Looking back, it's odd to me that he never wanted to continue playing when his marriage started to disintegrate. After our mother's death, Ben had the family piano shipped to Toronto, where it promptly fell apart.

RICHARD WAGNER, MAX REGER, KURT WEILL. Favourites. During the War, he would play Wagner loudly on the piano, aggravating Mr Babington, our very English neighbour. (We lived in a semi-detached house; a duplex.) In Oxford, he would again play Wagner, knowing it would aggravate his wife Herta, who preferred Robert Schumann. Reger: this composer was always too abstract for me; or was I just wanting to object to my father?

ALFRED DELLER. DD was the organizer of a conference at All Souls College, Oxford, and persuaded the famous countertenor to give a concert with Desmond Dupré. DD even negotiated a very reasonable fee.

༄

J. F. DAUBE. DD did know about Johann Friedrich Daube (c. 1730–1797), a lutenist and author of *The Musical Dilettante*,[29] but he told Matthew that he found out from someone outside the family. Johann Friedrich had converted to Christianity, and so was not mentioned within the family. Somehow I can't imagine DD playing the lute.[30]

༄

RECORDER. He played a Dolmetsch recorder, and I have pleasant memories of my mother accompanying him on the piano. Both the recorder and the piano seemed to disappear as his first marriage failed. He did not show much interest in a gramophone/phonograph/record player, but Ben remembers him proudly playing the *Dreigroschenoper* (*Threepenny Opera*) for Michael and himself when they visited him in his rooms at All Souls College.

༄

GROSSE BROCKHAUS. Whenever there was discussion at the dinner table, DD would go to the twenty-volume fifteenth edition of Germany's equivalent of the *Encyclopedia Britannica*, which came out between 1928 and 1935, i.e. (mostly) before the Nazi era. We have it in our house in Connecticut; ready for an interested grandchild or great-grandchild.

---

[29] J. F. Daube, *The Musical Dilettante: A Treatise on Composition*, trans. S. P. Snook-Luther (Cambridge 1992).

[30] I have bought a CD with J. F. Daube's music: Ireen Thomas, perf., *Herfstbloei van de Luit: Luitmuziek rond 1750* [Autumn Blossoming of the Lute: Lute Music around 1750], Buma ITH IV 1, 2000 [reissued 2002]. Ireen Thomas is also the author of *Catalogue of Contemporary Lute Music* (Utrecht 1986).

GIRLFRIENDS FROM THE THIRTIES. You want names? They include Karola Fettweis, whom Matthew and I met in Freiburg; Suzanne Dreifuss, whom Ben met in Zürich, and whom I visited shortly before her death; and Kaethe Zhao. Ms Zhao moved to China with her Chinese husband (when I do not know) and wrote on Chinese opera from a European perspective.

LOEB CLASSICAL LIBRARY. Even in wartime Cambridge, when DD had very little money, he would accumulate these books as they came out: Greek volumes cased in green, Latin in red; Latin or Greek on the left, English on the right. Given DD's stress on the importance of original texts, I am puzzled why he would want to own translations; never thought to ask him. His favourite, he said, was *The Golden Ass* by Lucius Apuleius, the only Latin novel to survive in its entirety. DD purported to enjoy its crudities. (See also the next item.)

GIOVANNI BOCCACCIO'S *THE DECAMERON*. Well known for its bawdy tales. I think DD read this in English rather than Italian.

SHAKESPEARE. Shakespeare was revered. And DD knew his Shakespeare. This should not surprise us: in his book *The Making of an Englishman*,[31] Fred Uhlman, author of *Reunion*,[32] painter, refugee and fellow-internee on the Isle of Man in 1940, wrote:

Shakespeare, together with Goethe and Schiller, was part of the German heritage, one of the rocks on which our education was based. Whatever the English may say about it, every German feels deep in his heart that Shake-

---

[31] London 1960.
[32] F. Uhlman, *Reunion* (London 1977).

speare was — or at any rate should have been — a German, and nobody in Germany would be surprised if somebody suddenly discovered that he really came from Weimar and not from Stratford-on-Avon. Few people over here probably realize how much of him has passed into the German language. Countless sayings of his are in common use: 'Ein Pferd, ein Pferd, mein Königreich für ein Pferd', 'es ist etwas faul im Staate Dänemark' . . . .[33]

DD would occasionally see a stage production or an Olivier film, but most of his knowledge came from intense and repeated readings of the texts. See DD's 'Shakespeare on Aliens Learning English': he must have written this in 1941, when nobody could be sure how the war was going and when the future was totally unpredictable.[34] He quotes Mowbray in *Richard the Second*, Act One, Scene Three, when he receives notice of exile for life:

> The language I have learn'd these forty years,
> My native English, now I must forgo.

DD knew whereof he wrote.

∽

DICKENS. Also revered. He told me of a man who couldn't bear to finish *The Pickwick Papers* because then it would be over.

∽

INHALATOR. Until his later years in California, DD's inhalator was his constant companion; his asthma bothered him every day. When DD, my mother and I went to Switzerland for six weeks in the late forties, we took the train through France, where I remember rationed yellow bread. When we got to Basel after a bumpy overnight ride, the customs official, seeing DD's inhalator, asked: 'Is this a bomb?' The question could have been serious. Matthew recalls DD asking him in

---

[33] Id., 197–98.
[34] See D. Daube, 'Shakespeare on Aliens Learning English', *Message — Belgian Review* (1942), reprinted in *Metamorphoses: A Journal of Literary Translation*, 6/2 (1998), 70, reprinted in C. Carmichael, ed., *Ethics and Other Writings* [*Collected Works of David Daube*, 4] (Berkeley 2009), 333–45.

the nineties to get a refill from Germany. He contacted the manufacturer, who informed him that they had not produced this type of inhalator in quite some time, although they did have a couple left on display in their company museum. Kathleen Vanden Heuvel writes:

> He still had this inhalator (complete with original instructions) at the Chaparral Nursing Home in Berkeley. He begged me to find him a replacement, as it was glass and was somewhat broken. I looked everywhere, contacting every medical device company I could find in the days before the web, which meant searching yellow pages for many cities. I could find no one who made the exact device, which he still wanted to use without the cartridges that were no longer manufactured. But I talked some guy into trying to recreate it with other pieces of equipment that he had. Needless to say, this did not please David at all. He was distressed that I could even imagine this newly constructed device was a suitable replacement for his beloved inhalator. The medical device guy explained to me that David's device could not help anyone to breathe, and I felt I had failed him. C'est la vie! I tried.

Bernard Jackson comments, 'He must have realized he was using it as a placebo (or for other purposes?).'

ORTHODOXY V. ORTHOPRAXY. Even when I was very young, I was told that, yes, I had to behave in certain ways — no carrying on the Sabbath, fasting as a firstborn the day before Passover,[35] etc. — but there was absolutely no pressure to believe anything. (Bernard Jackson points out that this was not unusual.) I had to spend untold hours learning Hebrew, but I was never ever asked to repeat, 'Hear, O Israel: the Lord is Our God, the Lord is One.' The family did not pray together. Maybe this is, in part, why I was never instructed by a rabbi. DD did teach me about the Seven Laws of Noah, the Noahide Laws: any non-Jew who lives according to these laws is regarded as a Righteous Gentile and is assured of a place in the world to come. The seven laws are prohibition of idolatry, murder, theft, sexual promiscuity, blasphemy and eating flesh taken from an animal while it is still alive; plus a requirement to have just laws.

---

[35] Which irked me, as I was the only firstborn in the house and missed out on special pre-Passover foods (potato salad with cut-up sausage: very tasty).

BAR MITZVAHS. All three sons' bar mitzvahs (one in Cambridge, two in Oxford) were carefully staged events, with many of DD's friends and colleagues present. Preparation took a couple of years, with daily half-hour pre-breakfast Hebrew lessons taught in German. Ashkenazi pronunciation, not Sephardi/Israeli. Synagogue service, with the bar mitzvah boy playing a major role; then lunch at Gonville and Caius or All Souls College. Immediately after the bar mitzvah, DD would lose interest in our development on the religious front. He left for his year-long 'world tour' the day after his youngest son's bar mitzvah. Come to think of it, DD didn't really know how to deal with children. He would, on occasion, haul me off for a mild beating with a stick that I still have — until Professor Buckland told him not to. From then on, he would occasionally 'confiscate' something of mine, and I could still point to the shelf in his cupboard where these things would linger.

SEDER. More theatre. During the forties and early fifties, DD would host the two seders (the two first nights of Passover) and my mother would provide the food: always matzo ball soup (Knödelsuppe), followed by another kind of matzo ball with the main course. He would invite some non-Jews to join us and would explain the rituals as he went through them. Black tie and evening dress *de rigeur*.

CHESS. DD was a pretty good chess player in his day, and had played against the famous grandmaster Aron Nimzovich. (Nimzovich escaped being drafted in 1917 by feigning madness, insisting that there was a fly on his head. DD must have enjoyed that.) My brother Michael would give him a run for his money. DD: 'I have played this like a fish.' He would often follow a newspaper chess game, and I can still recall the names of the world champions of his era: Emanuel Lasker,

José Raul Capablanca, Alexander Alekhine, Max Euwe and Mikhail Botvinnik. At the University of Aberdeen, DD was adviser to the chess club for a time. Matthew writes: 'One of the few personal items David kept in his bedside drawer in Konstanz was a book on chess and a travelling chess set.'

❦

CROSSWORDS. In the good old days, *The Observer* (London paper that comes out every Sunday; now sister paper of *The Guardian*) used to print two crosswords: Everyman (too difficult for me) and Ximenes (unbelievably hard). DD would do the Ximenes. DD told me on more than one occasion that he put together the first Hebrew-language crossword to be published in the United Kingdom: I wish someone could find it.

❦

DOGS. When DD boarded with the Misses Rose at 14 Montague Road, Cambridge, before he got married, he had a dog named Vakki. He wasn't especially interested in Curig (pronounced *kirrig*), the Welsh Springer we brought back from Capel Curig, North Wales.

❦

HANDWRITING. His Ds were oddly triangular.

❦

PENCILS. Unsharpened and short.

❦

SPELLINGS like 'shew'. Buckland used this variant, so that was good enough for DD. My *Concise Oxford Dictionary* describes it as 'old fashioned'.

❦

COLLEGE AND UNIVERSITY TIES. DD collected them, and my brothers and I have inherited a few, most of them ragged, but much better after being cleaned for the first time.

༄

BETS. Fellows of All Souls College used to bet (I don't know whether they still do) and I have seen the betting book where it is recorded that DD bet with Isaiah Berlin on the Eisenhower-Stevenson election. DD won.

༄

HUMPTY DUMPTY. 'The rhyme dates from the autumn of 1643. "Humpty Dumpty" is not an egg. It is a giant tortoise.'[36] DD was especially pleased when Beverley Cross wrote a libretto entitled *All The King's Men*,[37] which tells of the Siege of Gloucester of 1643 and the King's wonderful war machine, Humpty Dumpty.

> All the King's surgeons
> And all the King's wights
> Couldn't put Humpty Dumpty to rights.

The family has a letter headed 'The White House, Beaumont, near Wormley, Hertfordshire' which reads as follows:[38]

3 March, 1969

Dear Professor Daube,

It's a very long time since I was introduced to you by Brian Simpson of Lincoln [College] . . . . You may remember I most admired your account of the probable origins of 'Humpty Dumpty' . . . . Well, here it is — now in the form of a children's opera. It is to have its final performance in Coventry on March 29th, and I hope you'll have the chance to see it one day in Oxford.

Yours sincerely,

Beverley Cross

---

[36] See D. Daube, 'Nursery Rhymes and History', *The Oxford Magazine*, 74 (1956), 230–32, 272–74, 310–12, reprinted in C. Carmichael, ed., *Ethics and Other Writings* [*Collected Works of David Daube*, 4] (Berkeley 2009), 363–70.
[37] *All the King's Men: An Opera for Young People* (1968), libretto by Beverley Cross, music by Richard Rodney Bennett.
[38] Reproduced by permission of the Estate of Beverley Cross.

OLD TYPEWRITER RIBBONS. Ben says DD would collect them. Maddening, and without reason.

WARTIME REUSABLE ECONOMY LABELS. Also collected. Maddening, but with reason.

HITLER'S *BLACKLIST*. It was only after the war that DD discovered that he had been on a relatively short list of 2,300 persons who were to be arrested immediately when the Germans invaded Britain, which they expected to do[39] (and members of their families too!). Maybe if he had known, he would have been less dismissive of the idea of emigrating to the United States in the forties. He first learned of the existence of the *Blacklist* from the *London Evening Standard* after the war. He never knew why he was so honoured, since most of his Cambridge contemporaries were not on it. DD took particular pride in being on the same page as Lord Davies, who headed the economic boycott of Germany, and Lord Dawson of Penn, the King's doctor. Too late, in 1987, DD asked me why no one had bothered to organize a gathering of people on the list: that would, as he said in a letter, have been 'strange beyond belief'.

GENETICS. At Caius College, Cambridge, DD was befriended by Sir Ronald Fisher; at Oxford by Edmund Ford. And at Berkeley, influenced by both, he did some writing that in-

---

[39] The complete *Blacklist* is reprinted in two works: *Black Book: Sonderfahndungsliste G.B.* [Imperial War Museum, Facsimile Reprint Series, 2] (London 1989); Walter Schellenberg [SS-Brigadeführer], *Invasion 1940: The Nazi Invasion Plan for Britain*, ed. J. Erickson (London 2000).

volved genetics. Medical ethics was of increasing fascination to him.[40]

THE AFTERLIFE. DD was increasingly intrigued by the question whether there is life after death. He asked me once whether I believed that there was an afterlife; when I reluctantly said, 'No', he agreed, but with a sigh of regret.

SARGENES. I have vivid memories of DD wearing his sargenes under his tallith on Yom Kippur in the Cambridge synagogue. Orthodox male Ashkenazi Jews would wear this white linen garment, which would later serve as a shroud. As a small boy, I was impressed by the accompanying hat, which could be folded down to cover the face after death. DD was buried in his sargenes in California.

SWING LOW, SWEET CHARIOT. It was only recently (ten years too late) that I learned from Helen that DD loved this spiritual and wanted it sung at his funeral. It was written by Wallis Willis, a Choctaw freedman, some time before 1862.

PORTRAITS. There are two portraits of DD. There's a pastel hanging in the Main Hall at Yarnton Manor, Yarnton, Oxford, home of the Oxford Centre for Hebrew and Jewish Studies. The artist is Don De Mauro of Johnson City, New York, a member of the faculty at the State University of New York at Binghamton. The plaque reads:

---

[40] See C. Carmichael, ed., *Ethics and Other Writings* [*Collected Works of David Daube*, 4] (Berkeley 2009).

DAVID DAUBE

Presented on the occasion of his honorary LL.D. degree from Cambridge, June 11, 1981, by Alan Watson and Calum Carmichael.

Some years ago, DD sat for a portrait in Cambridge, Massachusetts, at my request, and the result is in our home in Manchester, Connecticut; there's a copy in the Law Library at the University of Aberdeen. The painter was Melvin H. (Mel) Robbins (1918–1999), many of whose portraits hang in the State House in Boston and at Harvard University.

∽

THE NUREMBERG TRIALS. DD always opposed them, believing strongly that a crime must be defined before you can be guilty of committing it, not after. Sir Hersch Lauterpacht, the distinguished Whewell Professor of International Law at Cambridge (1937–1955), was very much on the other side. ('Count me with Lauterpacht', writes Reuven Yaron.) I mention this in part because it was Lauterpacht who had advised DD to give up Roman Law and start on something else, since there was no future in it.[41] Sir Arthur Goodhart, Professor of Jurisprudence at Oxford and the first American to head an Oxford College (University College) was also in favour of the Nuremberg Trials:[42] interesting because DD at one time thought that it was Goodhart who recommended him for the regius chair.

(By the way: United States Chief Justice Harlan Fiske Stone called the Nuremberg Trials a fraud. I don't think DD knew this. And Associate Justice William O. Douglas wrote,

---

[41] DD recalled this when he received a handwritten letter from Prime Minister Winston Churchill asking whether he could recommend DD to Her Majesty the Queen for appointment to the Regius Chair of Civil Law at Oxford. I would give a lot to find that letter. And my brother Michael reminds me of DD's immense pleasure and pride when the official appointment was confirmed, along with the Royal Seal. When I had it framed shortly after DD's death, the framer gasped: the last document remotely like it that he had seen was a letter of appointment to the Governorship of Connecticut, dating from before the American Revolution.

[42] See A. L. Goodhart, 'The Legality of the Nuremberg Trials', *Juridical Review*, 58 (1946), 1–19.

'I thought at the time and still think that the Nuremberg Trials were unprincipled. Law was created *ex post facto* to suit the passion and clamor of the time.' According to British documents released in 2006, Churchill, in 1944, advocated a policy of summary execution in some circumstances, with the use of an Act of Attainder to circumvent legal obstacles. His mind was later changed by American leaders.)

❧

CLERIHEWS. Invented by Edmund Bentley near the beginning of the last century. DD was enchanted by their whimsical quality. At the Aberdeen dinner, I quoted two:

> George the Third
> Ought never to have occurred.
> One can only wonder
> At so grotesque a blunder.

and

> Moses Maimonides
> Wrote vast quantities
> And stood for amity
> In an age of calamity.

❧

GAUDIE. The weekly student newspaper at the University of Aberdeen. Still free. DD liked to be quoted.

❧

LOCUST. DD made a bet with Peter Stein in Aberdeen that he could introduce the word 'locust' into every single lecture in a series without the students suspecting anything. One time, he was making the point that different levels of formality are appropriate, depending on the topic and the setting of the conversation. For example, when his wife was serving dessert at 65 Osborne Place, it would be inappropriate for him to declaim, 'Lo! Custard!' I'm sure DD won the bet.

❧

TEACHING. In his Cambridge days, DD wanted to teach only advanced students and only Roman Law. By the time he got to California, he was enjoying teaching beginning students who had no Latin, and he had mastered the art of talking in fifty-minute bites. He was somewhat of a cult figure at Oxford, coming into his own at Berkeley. Needless to say, neither Jewish Law nor Roman Law was required there, and yet there were several years when DD attracted more students than anyone else (to the dismay of some of his colleagues). During the eighties we would discuss the art of teaching, each enjoying the perspectives of the other. His favourite teaching story: DD was explaining to a class how the ultimate gift is when the recipient does not know who the donor is.[43] Lo and behold, when he entered the lecture hall for the next class meeting, there, on the desk, was a large dish of his favourite ice cream: donor anonymous to this day. Needless to say, he ate it right there, and with relish.

Ken Walters[44] earned an A+ from DD at Berkeley, read the preceding paragraph, and wrote as follows:

> Much has been written about the significance of DD's writings, and much more work needs to be done to appreciate and document its significance. I wish there might also be a little article or 'collection of memories' focused on assessing and understanding DD's teaching brilliance. People mention humor, playfulness, showmanship – and those are valid but inadequate. In fact, to focus on these factors is in a sense unfair since it detracts from the substantive brilliance of what he brought to class each day. It was, to American students at least, new material. In each class, he was not only prepared; he was 'loaded' with 'great stuff'. Its freshness and relevance were apparent. Even the undergraduates at Berkeley were quite good and could not be seduced by mere showmanship and easy grades. I wish we knew more about your discussions with DD about teaching — you only mention them in passing . . . . We can indeed learn a great deal about teaching in seeing how DD crafted those lectures and presented them, and in the back-and-forth with students in and out of class; but he delivered the goods too. You learned a great deal in his classes.

ROMAN LAW. There was a time when every single Roman Law chair in the United Kingdom was held by one of DD's pupils.

---

[43] See R. Titmuss, *The Gift Relationship: From Human Blood to Social Policy* (Basingstoke 2002; orig. London 1970).
[44] See above, page 147.

I asked some people in the know whether anyone studies it today. David Ibbetson[45] responded:

In England it's still compulsory at Oxford and Cambridge (and both have an optional advanced course too); optional at Bristol and University College, London. I don't know of anywhere else that it is done at the moment, but since it depends very much on individual initiative it may have arisen elsewhere without my having heard of it. There was a lively course at Exeter until very recently, but I suspect that has lapsed with the retirement of its enthusiastic teacher. Cardiff likewise.

David Carey Miller[46] wrote:

What is significant about Scotland is that the Faculty of Advocates still require a credit in Roman Law and, of course, a good number of students want to keep their options open to practise at the Scottish Bar. Aberdeen students meet the requirement because our compulsory 'Foundations of Private Law' course — essentially Roman Law as relevant to Scots Law — is accepted by the Faculty of Advocates. The Aberdeen Chair of Civil Law has been vacant since the retirement in 2009 of Professor Gero Dolezalek. Certain other universities offer optional Roman law courses for students wanting to become advocates. Both Edinburgh and Glasgow are active in the scholarship of Roman law. Glasgow, of course, has the Douglas Chair of Civil Law, held since 2006 by Professor Ernest Metzger who formerly held a personal chair of Civil and Comparative Law at Aberdeen. Edinburgh's Civil Law chair remains unfilled but the Law School has a very active Roman Law Studies group which runs regular seminars. Dr Paul du Plessis, is course organiser of honours and ordinary courses in Civil Law.

Bill Gordon[47] wrote:

Roman Law is still compulsory in Aberdeen (. . . incorporated in an introductory course) and it is taught as an option in Dundee, Edinburgh and Glasgow. In Aberdeen, Edinburgh and Glasgow there are advanced or honours courses as well, and quite a few students come to Glasgow from Strathclyde and do the Roman Law course. Roman Law is still a requirement for those going to the Bar and an examination is set by the Faculty of Advocates for those who have not studied it in their degrees and thereby got an exemption from the Bar exam.

Ernest Metzger[48] wrote:

Roman law is thriving at the University of Glasgow. The introductory course, though optional, attracts large numbers from both the University of Glasgow and the University of Strathclyde. The honours-level course is naturally

---

[45] Regius Professor of Civil Law, University of Cambridge.
[46] See above, page 140.
[47] See above, note 10.
[48] Douglas Professor of Civil Law, University of Glasgow.

smaller but runs every year (apart from periods of academic leave). DD's works are extremely well-represented on the honours reading list.[49]

There is a Roman Law Group in London, and I am grateful to Andrew Lewis[50] for the following:

The Roman Law Group was founded by the late J. A. C. (Tony) Thomas in the late 1960s soon after he arrived at University College, London, as Professor of Roman Law. It was originally a gathering of UCL lawyers, including some non-Romanists. There was at the time a group meeting in Cambridge colloquially called the *gremium* and Tony would occasionally refer to the London meeting as the *grex*.

Tony deliberately made it a convivial as well as an academic occasion and the group regularly ate in the Spaghetti House off Goodge Street and the evening ended in a nearby pub. An early member around 1970 was Sue Hart, Tony's Ph.D. pupil, whose husband Colin, a criminal law barrister, came for dinner and acted as treasurer, collating the paying of the restaurant bill. The late Peter Birks was a member from when he came to UCL in the late 1960s. Tony Honoré was a regular visitor from Oxford. I did not join until 1973 when I came to UCL. By that time Peter Birks had gone to Brasenose (though he continued as a very regular member), two other early members had left, Paul Mahoney (who went to the Council of Europe) and Tony Oakley (who went to Cambridge).

The group met three times a year, during Tony Thomas's time always on a Thursday. After Tony's death in 1981, I took over the responsibility of running it and meetings moved to Fridays largely to avoid clashing with the Faculty's regular series of Current Legal Problem lectures on Thursdays. We nevertheless occasionally met on Thursdays to accommodate the needs of speakers.

The original pattern had been for the members to give regular papers, a formal act of business on each occasion being to nominate the next speaker, who was usually present. However, visitors were occasionally welcomed and I believe that your father was one such — though I think it must have been before 1973 as I think the only occasion on which I heard him speak at UCL was a meeting in the Hebrew department. After Tony's death, I was the only Romanist left in the Faculty and adopted a policy of inviting visiting speakers, though I myself, Peter Birks and Tony Honoré spoke regularly. It was at this time that the group was formally named the London Roman Law Group after a period when we had experimented with a group which rotated between London, Oxford and Cambridge. At least once a year we tried to attract a visitor from Europe. When Peter Birks moved to Edinburgh, he had started a Roman Law Group there which still continues to be very active.

During the 1990s, under the influence of the new Professor of Ancient History at UCL, Michael Crawford, more ancient historians began to be regu-

---

[49] 'The Three Quotations from Homer in Digest 18.1.1.1', *Cambridge Law Journal*, 10 (1949), 213–15; 'Certainty of Price', in D. Daube, ed., *Studies in the Roman Law of Sale* (Oxford 1959), 9–45; 'Utiliter agere', *IURA*, 11 (1960), 69–148; 'Condition Prevented from Materializing', *Tijdschrift voor Rechtsgeschiedenis*, 28 (1960), 271–96; 'Slightly Different', *IURA*, 12 (1961), 81–116; 'The Influence of Interpretation on Writing', *Buffalo Law Review*, 20 (1970), 41–59; 'The Self-Understood in Legal History', *Juridical Review* (n.s.), 18 (1973), 126–34.

[50] Professor of Comparative Legal History, University College London.

lar members. Alan Rodger also became a very supportive member and contributor. At the same time, although a wider circle of potential members joined the list of those receiving notices of meetings, most were at a distance from London and numbers of regular attenders began to fall off.

More recently with deaths and retirements of members it has proved hard to maintain regular meetings with sufficient numbers to justify inviting speakers and in the past couple of years the group has only met ad hoc when a visitor or member had a paper to communicate.

There is a Roman Law Group in Edinburgh, founded by the late Peter Birks around 1985 and presently run by Paul du Plessis. It meets three times a year and has a website.[51]

SCHOLARSHIP. Professor Paul Slack, Principal of Linacre College, a graduate college at Oxford that was founded in 1962, tells me that someone has given the money for a David Daube scholarship. The first recipient should be named next year.

SUCCESSORS AND PREDECESSORS. Aberdeen: DD was the first Professor of Jurisprudence. Successors: Peter Stein, Michael Meston, Geoffrey MacCormack and Robin Evans-Jones. Aberdeen created a separate chair of civil law at the beginning of this century: Cornelius van der Merwe, then Gero Dolezalek. At the time of writing, that post is vacant and being advertised. Oxford: Francis de Zulueta (1919–1948; even longer than Buckland's tenure at Cambridge),[52] Herbert Jolowicz, DD, Tony Honoré, Peter Birks and Boudewijn Sirks. Berkeley: DD was the first Co-Director of the Robbins Collection at the Law School at the University of California at Berkeley (Boalt Hall), along with Stephan Kuttner; they were followed by Laurent Mayali.

---

[51] The website of the Edinburgh Roman Law Group is accessible via the University of Edinburgh School of Law.
[52] 'Zulu', as DD called him, sold his personal library to the University of Aberdeen for a song. In 1953, the University honoured him with an LL.D., and he stayed in my room at 65 Osborne Place, teaching me how to pack a suitcase efficiently: I was fifteen and impressed.

GIFFORD LECTURES. DD was extraordinarily proud to have been asked to give the Gifford Lectures at the University of Edinburgh. Among postwar lecturers at the four ancient Scottish universities[53] were Niels Bohr, Gabriel Marcel, Michael Polanyi, Arnold Toynbee, Paul Tillich, Werner Heisenberg, Alister Hardy, Donald Mackinnon, Herbert Butterfield, Raymond Aron, Alfred Ayer, Hannah Arendt, Iris Murdoch, David Daiches, Carl Sagan, Antony Flew, Mary Warnock, Michael Dummett and Michael Ignatieff.

HONOURS. He enjoyed them! When he became a Fellow of the British Academy, he was especially pleased to be a member of three sections rather than one. Marion Paterson, Fellowship Officer at the British Academy, explains:

When Professor Daube was elected to the Academy in 1957, the Sections were slightly differently organized from the present. Professor Daube was primarily a member of the Jurisprudence Section (Section 8 as it was then), but as his scholarship also included biblical studies and ancient history, he was also a cross-member of these two Sections (Sections 3 and 1 as they were then).

He became a Fellow of the American Academy of Arts and Sciences in 1971.

Edinburgh was the first university to give DD an honorary degree (1960); then Paris (Sorbonne), Leicester, Munich, Hebrew Union College, Cambridge, Göttingen, Graduate Theological Union at Berkeley, Aberdeen (1990).[54] Plus an offer, in writing, from Neil Rudenstine, the President of Harvard, to which he felt he was no longer well enough to travel. So in Germany he would have had 'Dr. h.c. mult.' after his name, signifying several honorary doctorates.

---

[53] In order of founding: St Andrews, Glasgow, Aberdeen and Edinburgh.
[54] With acknowledgments to Geoffrey MacCormack, see *Aberdeen University Review*, 54/185 (1991), 65–67. Among other honorary graduates that year were Ted Hughes, the poet laureate; David Jenkins, Bishop of Durham; and Lord Wilson, then Governor of Hong Kong and now Chancellor of the University of Aberdeen.

FESTSCHRIFTEN. Three, not one: Roman Law, Jewish Law, New Testament.[55]

KONSTANZ. The University of Konstanz, on Lake Constance, was founded in 1965, and DD was a visiting professor there for many years. (They now have about nine thousand students.) He bought an apartment in the town, and put a mezuzah on the door at a time when he was no longer orthoprax. In response to a question, he told me how important it was to him to own a piece of Germany. I think I understood that. Needless to say, Konstanz is in *Baden*-Württemberg.

EAST BAY TERMINAL. DD would leave the house at 4.45 a.m., buy a cup of coffee and a donut, and take the 5.30 F bus to Berkeley. And the drivers and the cleaners would know him and chat with him. He would have walked the mile-and-a-half across town from Romolo Place to the Transbay Terminal.

TIPPING. Waiters across the world were impoverished by DD's death. His tips were extraordinary. Examples welcome. Ed Epstein[56] points out how, especially in his California years, DD would be what he calls a 'people collector'; he would invite groups of people to dinner at fancy restaurants, deliver lecturettes and enjoy lively discussions that ensued.

---

[55] A. Watson, ed., *Daube Noster: Essays in Legal History for David Daube* (Edinburgh 1974); B. Jackson, ed., *Studies in Jewish Legal History: Essays in Honour of David Daube* (London 1974); E. Bammel, et al., eds., *Donum Gentilicium: New Testament Studies in Honour of David Daube* (Oxford 1978).

[56] Edwin M. Epstein, Emeritus Professor at Berkeley, where he has taught since 1964. He was, over the years, DD's best friend at Berkeley who was not connected with his academic work.

SAN FRANCISCO CHRONICLE. I'm not clear why DD became an addict, since he had not been in the habit of reading newspapers. (Maybe, at Oxford, he skimmed some dailies at All Souls College.) Matthew writes, 'Perhaps, in part, because they carried *Dear Abby*, whereas the *San Francisco Examiner* carried what we agreed was the vastly inferior *Ann Landers*.' Kathleen Vanden Heuvel points out that he knew a surprising amount about current news — just by skimming the headlines. Even in his last years at Boalt Hall, he would make sure he had the right coins for his daily purchase. He would have been delighted when one of his students was quoted in a newspaper (the *Oakland Tribune*, not the *Chronicle*) after his death as saying, 'One of his key themes is that the ancients were as much sneaky liars, losers, failures, successes, generous, grandiose, colorful people as we are today.'

THE O. J. SIMPSON TRIAL. Even though he did not watch television, DD was quite well informed on the 1995 trial and, of course, had a point of view.

'WE KNOW VERY LITTLE.' A constant refrain. The older DD got, the more hesitant he became about how he stood on issues. And he loved to take arguments to logical extremes. Tina remembers DD talking about vegetarians' wish not to harm animals: 'But what about the bacilli?' quoth he.

'I'M IN A TERRIBLE STATE.' A tiresome refrain. Whenever one would call him on the telephone, these would be the first words out of his mouth. He was a hypochondriac. Not easy for those who were closest to him. An asthmatic most of his life, he might have taken better care of himself if he had known that he would reach the age of ninety.

SAN FRANCISCO EARTHQUAKE. I refer not to the earthquake of 1906, but rather to that of 5.04 p.m. on 17 October 1989. It was caused by a slip along the San Andreas Fault, lasted about fifteen seconds, killed 63, injured 3,757 and left 8,000–12,000 homeless. DD's senior daughter-in-law Linda will recall that the earthquake occurred minutes before the third game of the 1989 World Series, which coincidentally featured both of the Bay Area's Major League Baseball teams, the Oakland Athletics and the San Francisco Giants. Game Three was scheduled to start at 5.15 p.m. at Candlestick Park. This was the first major earthquake in America to be broadcast on live television. The San Francisco-Oakland Bay Bridge suffered relatively minor damage, as a fifty-foot section of the upper deck on the eastern side crashed onto the deck below. Police told drivers to turn around and drive back the way they had come. DD was on the F bus and, unperturbed, went back to his office at Boalt Hall, where he spent the night waiting for something to happen. I managed to get through to him before the electricity was cut off and the phones went dead, so I knew he was all right. I still marvel at his calm at that time.

'ES KANN ALLES AUCH ANDERS SEIN.' Supposedly Alfred Adler, the Austrian doctor and psychologist, would end some of his lectures with this saying: 'It can all be quite different.' Quirky fact: Adler died of a heart attack on Diamond Street, Aberdeen.

LIMERICKS. DD always loved limericks.[57] In the early eighties, I sent him a copy of *Limericks: Too Gross, or Two Dozen Dirty Dozen Stanzas* by Isaac Asimov and John Ciardi.[58] My accompanying note said, 'Do thou likewise.' And for several months I would get one or two limericks through the mail every few days, many of them elegant, some vulgar, some both. Participants in the Aberdeen conference were given a selection, prudently edited by David Carey Miller and his wife. (My brothers, son Matthew and I proudly retain the copyright.)

∽

DD would close a discussion with one or more of his sons with a German expression which meant 'Harrumph, I have spoken!' He thought he was quoting the King of the Apes (the expression 'I have spoken' appears frequently in the Tarzan stories of Edgar Rice Burroughs) but he was in fact quoting Winnetou, the Chief of the Mescalero Indians in the writings of Karl May. DD used it when he had had enough disputation. So in the spirit of DD at his best, and also at his most ornery —

HUK, ICH HABE GESPROCHEN

---

[57] When I was growing up in Cambridge, his favourites were:

> There was a young man of Khartoum
> Who kept two black sheep in his room.
> He said they remind me
> Of one left behind me,
> But I cannot remember of whom.

and

> There was a young man of Japan
> Whose poetry never would scan.
> When asked why it was,
> He said, 'Well, because
> I always try to get as many words into the last line as I possibly can.'

[58] New York 1978.

www.ingramcontent.com/pod-product-compliance
Lightning Source LLC
LaVergne TN
LVHW041620070426
835507LV00008B/347